HAPPILY I
FOR GR

GU00457050

*A non-fairytale, post-wedding,
blues-busting guide for newlyweds:*

A success coach's perspective

Gina Visram

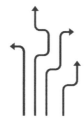

Four Arrow Publishing

About the Author

Gina Visram is a career development coach, who as part of her 'Limitless Coaching' initiative, works with clients to help them maximise or regain focus and drive to achieve key goals. UK-based but with life and educational experience of Guyana, Montserrat, Barbados, Kenya and now the UK, Gina brings a relatable, global and multi-cultural perspective to the field of coaching.

After nearly seven years in the communications field with global organisations including Pearson Plc, BBC World and CNBC, Gina embraced career coaching as her vocation. She formed Limitless Coaching after qualifying as a coach through The Coaching Academy, the largest coach training organisation in the world. Her clients describe her remarkable ability to identify issues and fears about their life and work and coach them through.

Gina is emerging rapidly as a lead moderator and facilitator in discourse on the traditionally "hushed" subject of 'post-wedding blues'. A relative newlywed herself, Gina married on 29 April 2011, the most anticipated wedding day of a generation, thanks to the nuptials of Britain's Prince William & Kate Middleton on that same day. Gina is keen to point out, however, that she and fiancé chose that date more than six months before they did!

The trigger for her focus on 'post-wedding blues' was perhaps that Gina herself, sensed a slump in personal motivation immediately after her wedding. This felt unusual, unsettling and unsustainable - and she was determined to see whether any other newlyweds had experienced something similar. They had; as she found out after interviews with many, hence her focus on newlyweds in her coaching workshops, crafting her signature "HAPPILY" coaching system and writing the book "Happily Ever After for Grown-Ups".

Gina earned an undergraduate degree in Politics, International Studies & Gender from the University of Warwick and an MA in International Journalism (with Distinction) from Cardiff University; and accreditation with The Coaching Academy.

To stay in touch with Gina, follow her on Twitter @ bridemotivation – and enquire about working directly with her at any time, through Facebook page "Happily Ever After for Grown-Ups" www.facebook.com/happilyever afterforgrownups and her website www.limitlesscoaching. com.

Praise for
"Happily Ever After for Grownups"

"I wish this book was available when I got married 7 years ago, as I recognise how I felt just a few months after my wedding. Gina's effective strategies and advice will help you to get back on track, re-find your mojo, and, most importantly, learn how to do this effectively as a couple."

—Karen Williams, Business Coach

"Planning a wedding can consume your mind and thoughts for months before your big day, however when it's all over some brides may feel as if they're missing something or may feel the need to focus on something new. Happily Ever After for Grown Ups can help newlywed couples create a new focus as they commence a successful journey in life together."

—Francesca Cribb, Site Editor, hitched.co.uk

"With great understanding Gina Visram shares some important insights for newlyweds and recently-weds how to successfully transition into married life with deft practicality whilst focusing on values, communication and your own identity."

—Roberta Jerram, UK serial entrepreneur and married mum of 4.

"Happily ever after for grown-ups is a must read for any woman who has ever experienced a motivational slump or simply wants to get more out of her everyday life. With advice from experts, stories from other women, and exercises to help you put your new learnings into practice, you will discover you are not alone and that it is possible to achieve everything you've ever wanted - in your personal life, career and most importantly your relationship/marriage. The book is a lovely combination of fun and humour alongside real tools and techniques that will help you kick your own butt out of that dip and towards success.

—Kaneen Morgan, Business Owner

"It's funny, I would have never thought I was the type to need 'motivating'. But after reading just a few chapters of this book, I realised I was stuck in a rut and that the 'honeymoon was over'. I went back to work that same week having made some clear goals in my life and things started happening! A few weeks later I got a promotion at work and a 30% salary increase, which will definitely help to pay off the wedding!"

—Fariba Soetan, Policy Advisor

From the start it's a fantastically personal journey, which through Gina's quick wit and fluid style, kept me smiling for hours afterwards!

The first chapter fuelled hedonistic nostalgia and got me right back to thinking about the most wonderful day of my life (with a goofy grin on my face to match!). I only wish I would have seen the second chapter before my wedding!

What Gina really helps put into perspective is the normality of what many newlyweds (myself included) consider to be a bit of a motivational dip after the wedding. The tone is conversational, clear and practical and it's great to know these words come from someone with first-hand experience - the lady really knows what she's talking about!

The opening chapters have already helped me to begin evaluating my own wedding journey and pointed out some of the things I only wish I'd have known beforehand. These clearly delineated pointers could have helped me stay on the crest of the wedding-day-bliss-wave for far longer, and avoid the slippery slope to the 'post-wedding blues'.

—Stacy Moore, Educational Psychologist

First published in 2013 by Four Arrow Publishing
A division of Limitless Coaching Ltd.

Copyright © Gina Visram 2013

Four Arrow Publishing

c/o 36a Rosebery Close
Morden, Surrey, SM4 4NR
United Kingdom

E-mail: gina@limitlesscoaching.com

ISBN 978-0-9575616-0-1

British Library Cataloguing in Publication Data
A catalogue record for this book is available from the British Library

Cover designed by Cathi Stevenson of Book Cover Express

Cover photo by Tamsin Watson

Typeset in Adobe Garamond Pro by JustYourType.biz

Printed and bound in Great Britain by York Publishing Services

To the amazing examples of individuals and couples who balance career and personal success – and to all the newlyweds who recognise that creating your own personal fairytale involves work and dedication. I respect you all and wish you the luck, love and career and personal success you seek.

Contents

Chapter 1 – Introduction 21

How will this book help you? 21

What is the post-wedding blues? 23

My story.. 24

Fit for a princess! 27

The day arrived 28

The inspiration behind this book................... 32

Chapter 2 – **H**and on Heart–The Self-Audit Chapter: It's

all about me me me 37

So what is a self-audit? 38

Hello… my name is….. 40

What's in a name? 42

Real bride reflection experiences..................... 46

So what does all of this mean?......................... 50

Chapter 3 – **A**ims & Goals: Be a Goal-Setting Queen......... 53

Common goal-setting occasions 54

What is a goal?... 55

A guide to effective goal setting...................... 57

Make your goals SMART.. 60

Goal setting theory and approaches

beyond SMART... 76

Chapter 4 – **P**eople Power: Re-establish your networks.... 81

Networking: Personal 84

Networking: Professional 92

Networking: Social... 99

Chapter 5 – **P**artnership: Strengthen your union 103

What is marriage? 105

Keeping fun alive 114

Time management and togetherness 118

Chapter 6 – **I**nvestigate your career:

Do a Career Audit 129

Work/life perspectives from real brides 137

Your values and beliefs 157

How to approach you boss about a

promotion 166

Top tips for job hunting in any job

market 170

Chapter 7 – **L**ove, laugh and communicate:

Set your own rules of communication 181

Tips for effective communication in the early

days of marriage 182

Communications challenges and

triumphs of newlyweds 196

The new communications rules 203

Chapter 8 – **Y**our strength in numbers:

Share Experiences 213

Chapter 9 – Meet the contributors 227

Chapter 10 – Next Steps 237

Acknowledgments

Writing this book has been a real labour of love (and sometimes a test of how well I can balance a range of demanding things in my life!) and I am so grateful to everyone who has been part of the journey in one way or another.

Firstly, I must thank my husband. Rahim, you are everything I wanted and more in a husband and I couldn't ask for a better partner in crime! In fact, it was my awareness of how truly happy I am to be in this partnership with you that made me realise something [external to us] was up when I felt a bit deflated at times following our gorgeous wedding day(s). The confidence that I have about the two of us led me down the path of researching sources of the malaise, fatigue and demotivation I sometimes felt when we got back to post-wedding normality… and the result was not only a process of self-discovery but was also the concept and now completion of this book which will hopefully resonate with women around the world.

Thanks also to my parents – Donna Ramsammy James and Carlton James – a couple of awesome individual personalities that have been together over 40 years and married over 35. Collectively, you are the source of my early understanding of teamwork, adventure, bravery, confidence and love. Mum… thank you so much for being my biggest cheerleader, critic (when needed) and confidant. Dad… thank you for being such a great example of many things including communications at its best. From your on-air broadcasting mastery to your ability to effectively communicate with people from every conceivable walk of life – you have been instrumental in helping me recognise my own voice.

There is something incredibly powerful about parents who consistently make it clear to their children that their dreams are within their reach, if they keep working towards them. It is often your voices of encouragement I heard when my attempts to balance writing this book with a demanding full time job and other commitments sometimes felt overwhelming.

Thanks to the experts involved including entrepreneur Penny Power for the heartfelt foreword – and Karen Williams, Bella (of Rareworld); Erin Tillman (The Dating Advice Girl); The Social Media Couple (The Krafskys) and many more for writing bespoke content or allowing me to reproduce existing material.

To Stacy and Fariba, you ladies have been amazing. While balancing your full time jobs, relationships and roles as mothers / mothers-to-be – you took the time to read the book as chapters became available. Your feedback has been invaluable in making the final product what it is. I hope you're proud of it too!

Essentially, I would like to express my gratitude to everyone who joined me on the journey through this book. Thanks to all those who provided support, were interviewed, participated in impromptu brainstorms, copy edited, proofread and designed. A huge thank you to Paula Charles and the team at York Publishing Services for being the all-important final stage of turning the content into this final product I am so proud of.

As you read through the book it quickly becomes clear that this is not the work of one person in isolation but features the contribution of many. My final sentiment is HUGE thanks to the brides (both newlywed and 'established-wed') and a groom (thanks!) who took the time to share experiences. Any doubt any of us ever held about the power of strength in numbers has hopefully now diminished as these very personal stories of women from Kenya to Canada; the USA to India and Germany to the UK are shared. In this very fast paced world we live in where it can be tough enough to manage whatever you have going on that day, I am grateful for the time, honesty and beauty of each one of your experiences. The richness of this book is enhanced by you.

Thank you.
Gina Visram

Foreword

Gina asked me to share my marriage experience with you for the foreword to this book. That is extremely flattering. It is not extraordinary as a marriage, but it works and it is my greatest success and I am grateful for the stability and anchor it has been in my sometimes turbulent life. My hope is that my openness here will touch some of your hearts as you go through your marriage. This is real life, not Mills and Boon, and not Hollywood.

On July 7th 1990, I married my soul mate. We had been dating for only 13 months and I knew on the day we first dated, 5th May 1989 he was the man I wanted to grow old with, have children with and spend as much of my waking hours and sleep with. I was so lucky. Nearly 23 years later, I still feel that way. I am a very lucky lady. We now have 3 children aged 20, 18 and 15, a close family and still our sanity.

Has it been easy? To love, yes, to cope with the ups and downs of life, no. The 23 years have had their challenges, been exhausting at times, moments of fearing the credit card at the supermarket, moments of ridiculous workload, moments of love and possibly the odd moment of dislike. We have some things in common and some things that we are have different views on. That is life, how can you possibly be with someone for so long and not have challenges.

For the past 15 years we have worked together in business, allowing us to share the joys, inspiration, glory and at times the work load. We are a team when it comes to the work, children and home. I am a complete control freak with regard to the kids, I dominate (or try to) all the discipline, educational decisions and present buying. We have quite strong demarcation of roles, in fact despite us sharing the responsibility of income, I always thank Thomas for our meals out, holidays and treat him as the main breadwinner, and so do the children. I got into a tussle with Vanessa Feltz on her Radio Show when I told her that fact - very un-modern. I like it that way. I like my man to be manly; I like to feel looked after.

Our marriage has never been a competition, we have never completed at who is most exhausted and who is contributing the most. Life is ying and yang, we flow, sometimes it is my time to shine, sometimes it is Thomas'.

Marriage to me is a partnership in life, a place where I believe it is my role to make Thomas happy that he married me and I try to earn that praise and respect daily by my actions. I do not believe it is his job to make me happy though, and I know he doesn't believe it is mine to make him happy. Happiness is your own state of mind, so is tenacity, determination and staying power. We see the long term and long term I want to grow old with him and so we overcome challenges and never see an exit.

We are lucky, we have not had any serious adversity, no serious pain or challenges, but we have had many years of financial strain, exhausting times with children, months without sex through lack of energy and time and times when we barely have a chance to talk about anything other than work. Sometimes Thomas is the father of my children, sometimes he is my business partner and when I am very lucky he is my husband. As we grow old, he and I will be husband and wife more often, and that will be wonderful, for now we dedicate ourselves to our family and our business partners and the teams of people around us, tomorrow we can dedicate ourselves to one another, and my prayer is that we both live long enough for those twilight years.

So, Gina has dedicated her time to bringing this book to newlyweds starting their journey and I guess I have shared openly here that life is a journey, no rush and we don't have to achieve everything in our first 10 years. We do have to love one another, that is a choice you make and it is free to do. Your state of mind is your choice and if you manage your mind you can manage anything that life throws at you.

I wish you a life-time of love and happiness, find your own way, and be happy with the person you have dedicated the rest of your life to.

Penny Power,
January 2013

chapter **1**

Introduction

I consider myself to be lucky in love (and if you are reading this book, there's a chance that it means you are too). I recently married the man of my dreams – and am now enjoying life as a newlywed.

So what comes next?

In fairytales, this is the part where the story always ends with the rosy idea 'and they lived happily ever after…'

This is a lovely notion when you are nine years old, but when you are 24, 29, 33, 38, 42 or whatever age you are when you marry your other half, the chances are that you need a little more detail than that. Why? Our life experience brings us to the point where we realise that relationships – even fabulous passionate newlywed ones – need work, investment, shared goals, solid communication and much more, if that 'happily ever after' is ever to come to fruition.

Grimm's Fairytales (or indeed the Walt Disney Studios adaptations we are familiar with) include childhood favourites Sleeping Beauty, Cinderella, Snow White and the Seven Dwarfs, and more. While they may have been set in different kingdoms, all have one thing in common – the tale ends when the princess and the prince get together.

In a non-Disney world however, finding your Prince Charming is just the beginning, as lying ahead is a lifetime of adventure… celebrations, commiserations, extraordinary occasions and, let's be honest, a whole lot of humdrum day-to-day existence.

If you are recently married, I would wager that a major milestone for you was your wedding day and you are not the only one. Popular culture suggests that most women expect their wedding to be the best day of their life. This is one of the reasons that some newlyweds experience post-wedding depression, post-wedding blues or less severely, some kind of post-wedding dip in motivation. Please note, I am not qualified to discuss depression and recommend that if suffering any kind of depression, wedding-related or not, you should consult your GP immediately. It is the latter two, post-wedding blues and dips in motivation, that I'll be exploring in this book.

How will this book help you?

The period leading up to a wedding and subsequent marriage is a time of reflection. Therefore, this book will give you an insight into how best to transition into this new stage of your life in the best way for you as an individual and also for you as part of a couple. It will also explore what is commonly known as the post-wedding blues. As you work through the chapters, I will show you tools and tactics to help you establish what actions and decisions *you* can take to create the kind of life *you* want:

- If you are recently married – this book will equip you with the tools you need to snap out of it and return back to being 'you'

- If not yet married – it will give you insights into what to look out for, and advance notice of actions you can take now to ensure you minimise the potential effects of any post-wedding blues.

It's important that life doesn't just happen to you. You have the power to create the experience that you want, so the more tools you have at your disposal, the more power you have to get on with the happily ever after you are destined for.

What is the post-wedding blues?

Psychotherapist Phillip Hodson describes the post-wedding blues as the moment a couple/newlyweds "discover there is no happy ever after." He says "the flat feeling, coupled with the financial hangover from the wedding can bring on a bout of post-nuptial blues."

A fellow of the British Association for Counselling and Psychotherapy, he claims that as many as one in ten women suffers from post-nuptial depression (PND) and notes that many brides place too much expectation on what marriage will bring them. In agreement with observations earlier in this book, he declared "There is no happy ever after... weddings are an out-of-date ritual that offer nothing concrete to the modern independent woman but are still sold as an answer to every dissatisfaction she might have with her life."

He states PND is on the increase and "ranges from vague discontent to full-scale depression. Left untreated it can go on indefinitely, getting more ingrained." While it has also been known to affect grooms, he says "Women are more likely to be affected as they tend to have a stronger emotional investment in marriage."

Maybe my vision is still in the newlywed rose-tinted perspective, but I do not agree with the point that weddings are out of date and only lead women to dissatisfaction with their everyday lives. I believe that wedding celebrations have a lot to offer the modern couple and indeed the modern woman. The idea of a celebration, complete with your closest friends and family, marking the beginning of a marriage is not a tradition I think will ever go out of style. Nonetheless, his definitions and research about the post-wedding blues and PND are generally helpful in the context of this book. And it was actually my own experience of a touch of the post-wedding blues which led me to explore the topic more and write this book.

That said, it is important to state that my expertise is as a newlywed and a certified personal performance coach. My role is to provide the tools and knowledge you need to move forward effectively when feeling unmotivated. I am not a psychotherapist and will not analyse any specific symptoms of PND. Instead, this book is about regaining your mojo… and at the end of each chapter, you will have specific tools and exercises to help you do just that.

Before I get into the detail of the steps which help multitasking newlyweds achieve post-wedding productivity, let me share my story so you can understand how I got to where I am now.

My story

My husband and I got married on what was arguably the most famous wedding day of a generation – Friday, 29

April 2011 – the same day as Prince William and Kate Middleton's royal wedding. Just to be absolutely clear… we picked the date first!

Following our beautiful engagement in 2009, we planned our wedding within 16 months. Although it is often said that your wedding day is the best day of your life, I almost didn't think that we'd be able to top the day he proposed. This was just under three years into our relationship and the notion of marriage was nothing new. In fact, we discussed marriage after eight months of getting together as we were house hunting and mutually agreed that we were heading in that direction before we decided to buy a home together.

Do you remember the stage in your relationship when you knew… for sure… that the two of you were meant to be together?

Mine came on our first holiday, in Marrakech, a mere five months after getting together. I remember being surprised at how certain I felt about this partnership, less than six months into it.

Years later, I admit secretly hoping he'd pop the question at varying points before he actually did. We shared a number of 'perfect occasions' where he didn't propose but I knew that if I kept thinking that way I would make myself crazy, so I banished these thoughts from my mind.

Proposal speculation officially parked in an inaccessible part of my brain, when we arrived at my parents' house in Guyana in December 2009, we were looking forward to a week of festivities and relaxation. Well, that was my agenda. Rahim had other plans… plans that I was completely oblivious to until Christmas morning after the four of us had opened all of our presents by the tree, and he suggested we split a Christmas cracker.

It was when the cracker went pop and the small dark blue box came flying towards me that I realised this was the present I'd been looking forward to for a while – and I was not disappointed! The box contained a present tag with the words "Will you marry me" emblazoned on it and a gorgeous sparkling diamond solitaire ring.

Fast forward about eleven months to November 2010 and the nation was celebrating the engagement of the future King to his university sweetheart, Kate Middleton. Six months earlier, Rahim and I had decided on our date and booked our Windsor venue. So, when the royals announced that they'd be tying the knot on Friday, 29 April 2011, we realised that the exciting countdown which every engaged couple enjoys would be magnified to the umpteenth degree as the world's media would be counting down with us.

Within three months of the royal couple getting engaged, it became clear that I was right. The incessant media countdown meant that we knew when there was a hundred days remaining, three months remaining and so forth. Fittingly, I began a blog, mostly to vent about the pressure of the world's media constantly speaking of our day. Here's one example.

Fit for a princess!

Posted on February 10, 2011 by
royalweddingcountdown

On Monday, ITV's Daybreak told me that there were twelve weeks until my wedding. Well, this national UK breakfast programme wasn't acting as my personal diary, but they said it was twelve weeks until the royal wedding… and while I've never considered myself to be a princess (I even disliked anything pink and girly when I was a kid), I have decided that if ever there's a time to embrace the 'princess' side all of us girlies possess… it's when the future King and Queen of England have decided they are getting married on the same day you are!

It seems Friday, 29 April 2011, the day my fiancé and I decided on nearly a year ago in April 2010, is one fit for a princess.

This incessant media countdown however may be more of a help than a hindrance as I am finding myself awake at all hours – remembering things that need to be done and furiously scribing them in my trusty notebook.

As a success coach and PR professional, I am no stranger to effective event planning and organisation – but I realised this week that if the media is going to keep publicly counting down to my (well of course 'our') big day… I may as well return the favour and keep them posted about what I'm doing too.

Thus… the royalweddingcountdown blog was born…

"If you can't beat 'em join 'em" they say… and that blog entry is representative of my state of mind, just three months away from the wedding we'd been planning for about a year. While in theory, we had the bulk of the organisation done (ie, venue confirmed, menu chosen, photographer booked, dress bought and paid for, colour scheme decided, groomsmen lined up for their fitting and much more), I still had what seemed like thousands of ideas, plans, goals, flashes of inspiration and every-thing in between jostling for space in my head.

The blog became a release… because I can assure you that even for the calmest, most organised bride, a con-stant countdown from the world's media and incessant wedding-related chat, becomes tiresome as the pressure begins to seep in.

What did you do to relax from your wedding planning stress?

Looking back, I can see that I didn't think the world revolved around me, had no sign of cold feet, was defi-nitely not panicky and had not fallen into the trap of wanting everything to be 'just so' (i.e. with an uncom-promising view of a 'perfect' day that we were trying to create). However, like most brides, I was still so focused on creating the best possible day for us and our guests that I can now see how I became susceptible to a touch of the post-wedding blues.

The day arrived

As the gorgeous strings section came to a close, and the sultry sound of one of soul's most arresting and memorable voices, Etta James, filled the room, it felt like the beginning of the rest of my life and a culmination of over a year of planning.

This moment, the moment where my dad was walking me down the aisle towards my husband-to-be was what all the months of planning had been about.

> *"At Last... my lo-o-ove has come along*
> *My lonely days are over*
> *And life is like a song*
> *At last...*
> *The skies above are blue*
> *My heart was wrapped up in clover*
> *The night I looked at you..."*

As my dad slowly walked me up the aisle, making sure not to step on my beautiful ivory lace-trimmed gown, I looked around the room at the smiling faces of all our family and friends who had made the journey to come and be a part of our special day. I also looked at my then fiancé – the man who was about to promise to love me and cherish me, forsaking all others, in sickness and in health for the rest of our lives. *That* is not a small promise... and not one that either of us took lightly. A Hollywood type 72 day marriage, this was not to be!

As my right hand was gently transferred from my dad's hand to that of my husband-to-be, I was pleased to see the tell-tale signs that his emotional state matched mine. The joyous smile of happiness, the slight emotional tremble of his hand and his teary eyes matched my feelings entirely.

Like I am sure yours was/will be, our whole ceremony was a joy. From the hilarity of the bridal party dancing (yes… literally dancing) down the aisle to the legendary sounds of Lionel Richie in the 80s (a track called *My Destiny*) to the moments when my groom fluffed his lines – unintentionally disregarding the words of the registrar and instead replacing every other word with 'love' instead of the suggested pledge. From the delivery of a poem which describes the ingredients for love in baking terms… to what seemed like forever spent pretending to sign the register. It was on this note of commitment and merriment that we wanted to start our marriage.

And so we did.

The evening reception, held at the same venue, kicked off with the tropical sounds of steel pans and the clinking sound of ice as homemade Guyanese rum punch was poured into tall glasses and circulated. Our guests gathered around the marquee – soaking up the mild April sunshine while my new hubby and I started the customary photography process.

Even as the day was unfolding, I began to understand why people refer to this day as the best of your life.

Hundreds of snaps later, we entered the reception marquee to rapturous applause, which while loud, was not enough to conceal the acknowledgement of my new identity… "We welcome Mr and Mrs Visram".

After twenty-nine years of being Miss James, Gina, Gina G, Gina J, DJ GJ (the latter harking back to my university radio show days), or any other such combination you could fathom – to me, this new title was quite a development. While I did not want to lose the identity I had proudly built up over the past (nearly) three decades, this made everything official… and represented the culmination of all the planning and indeed the lifelong commitment we were making to each other.

And so our married life began – amidst 180 or so of our closest family and friends and one helluva party. It soon became clear – *this* is the reason why so many couples spend tens of thousands on their big day. R and I had made the decision early in our planning that when it came to investment in our wedding, we would rather a less special venue and the ability to include/invite as many friends and family as possible – as opposed to a stunning venue where we could only afford a handful of guests. Lucky for us we came up trumps because as we surveyed the splendour of the Royal Windsor Racecourse, there wasn't anywhere we would have rather been (and that includes on Channel 4's *Million Pound Drop* programme but more about that later.)

My husband and I met in a London club in 2007 (apparently you really can meet the person of your dreams on a night out), and dance had never been far from us as a couple.

So what better way to pay tribute to the unifying force in our relationship than having a dance theme at our wedding reception? This wasn't just a case of boogieing until the wee hours of the morning, but was our ode to this art form. Instead of having a receiving line at the beginning of the reception where we greeted our guests, or even a plan to walk around each table over the course of the evening, we decided to take the dance theme beyond the cute dance names for each table.

We created a 'greet each table' game which involved dancing with each table individually, to the type of music cited in their table name... a soundtrack of global, culturally-representative genre-changing music – from the energetic sounds of *soca* to the varied paced traditional Greek Syrtaki (*Zorba*) music... and the timeless sounds of the waltz to hand-raising *bhangra* beats. As we hit a crescendo with popular Caribbean music, we could only smile and thank our lucky stars because for us, this was the blessing, the way to begin married life.

And we didn't stop there! Three days later we flew out to Guyana to celebration number two at my parents' home. Entirely organised by my mum, this ceremony was minimal stress for us, and it was incredible to have another opportunity to celebrate our union with family and friends around the globe.

So now you know my journey to the pinnacle of wedding day happiness, let me share with you what happened next.

The inspiration behind this book

After the fantastic wedding events I've just described, I felt a temporary low although I knew we would have years of excitement ahead. As is the case for many brides, months and months of planning culminated into what is commonly branded 'the best day of my life' so is it shocking to experience a temporary slump in motivation levels?

What did this post-wedding motivation slump look like?

Well, I'm the kind of person that friends always buy pamper and relaxation packs because they think I'm constantly on the go; so at first, I didn't worry too much about slowing down a bit. I suppose I decided that after such a long period of constant organising and planning, I deserved to give myself a couple of weeks of doing the bare minimum, ie, going to and from work, enjoying a *Zumba* or belly-dance class here and there... and not feeling compelled to take on a new project or re-establish attempts to build my coaching business.

Wedding planning can be strenuous and emotional for those involved, and I do think brides and grooms deserve a break after such a massive event. However, when two weeks off became four and four weeks became six, I became slightly concerned – and realised I needed to snap out of the slump I seemed to be in.

And who better to snap me out of my reverie than Tony Robbins, world-leading life coach, entrepreneur, author and peak performance strategist himself. This wasn't a case of listening to an audio recording. I had signed myself up for an event called the *National Achievers Congress* which featured inspirational business speakers including Tony Robbins, Richard Branson and Sir Alan Sugar. It took place about six weeks after we had returned to London and it was at this event that I literally felt my fatigue slipping away and my natural kick-butt, motivated, positive attitude come back to the fore...

... and how I'd missed it.

But when it was back, it was back with a vengeance. Not only did I finish the weekend having signed up for an internet marketing programme to boost my business and that of my husband, but the idea for this book came to me and I made the decision to write this book.

So how does this affect you?

Well, in this day and age when we are so time poor, it would be a real waste to spend time reading a book like this written by someone you don't feel like you engage with. This is why I have shared my experience, allowing you to recognise any similarities you may have.

As well as being a lucky-in-love-royal-wedding-day-sharing newlywed, I am also a certified personal performance coach. Following my own experience, I was determined to put together a coaching programme that could help people to minimise or even altogether avoid the post-wedding blues.

I only self-diagnosed this as the source of my fatigue after speaking to a number of women who genuinely resonated with this slump in motivation after their big day. In describing my experience, I have been met with understanding, relief, new-found clarity, empathy, sisterhood, camaraderie, unity and more – and the constant surprise that no one talked about this.

So here I am.

I again emphasise that this is not a book about post-nuptial depression (a very real condition for some newlyweds for which I would recommend seeking the support of a GP).

This book instead offers the framework of a bespoke coaching system to help achieve a relationship / career balance post-wedding... especially for those that need a bit of post-wedding motivation. By following the H.A.P.P.I.L.Y system detailed in the steps listed below, I will help you get back to your productive best:

1. **H**and on heart - Do a self-audit (i.e. get to know yourself)
2. **A**ims & Goals: Become a goal-setting queen
3. **P**eople Power: Re-establish your networks
4. **P**artnership: Strengthen your union
5. **I**nvestigate your career: Do a career audit
6. **L**ove, laugh and communicate: Set your own rules of communication
7. **Y**our strength in numbers: Share experiences.

My request to you? To use the system effectively, read the first three chapters in sequence and complete the related exercises. After that, go through the other stages in any order that suits you as they are self-contained.

Peppered between these steps to *Happily Ever After for Grown-ups,* you will find memorable marriage definitions, top tips about changing your look and increasing your self-confidence, secrets from wedding experts and the all-important stories from brides. Brides of varying cultures based all over the world. Some newlyweds. Many who wholly experienced the post-wedding blues. Some who didn't. All of whom, like you, are fabulous.

Chapter 2

Hand on Heart—The Self-Audit Chapter: It's all about me me me!

Promise to cherish, honour and be faithful... to yourself.

If you are a newlywed or about to be, you are hopefully basking in the glow of your recent or upcoming celebrations. Forming a commitment with the person of your dreams does not happen every day, so savour every moment!

However, once vows have been exchanged, the best man has given his cringe-worthy speech, your gorgeous gaggle of bridesmaids have done you proud, the multitiered cake has been cut, the first dance has been waltzed and essentially, the biggest party you will ever throw is over and you are back from your once-in-a-lifetime honeymoon extravaganza... *this* is the time to recognise the importance of being you!

That's right. You. Not just the new you who is a new wife, but the old you who is the woman your husband fell in love with. The one who always had a funny tale to tell after a night out with the girls and had crazy gossip to share after a day at the office. It is important for you to re-acquaint yourself with the pre-wedding planning you... the woman who shook it at *Zumba* twice a week and visited out of town friends once every few months.

So how do you reincorporate thinking about you-specific things after solely thinking about 'we' for countless months?

You conduct a self-audit.

So what is a self-audit?

The general definition of an *audit* is an evaluation of a person, organisation, system, process, enterprise, project or product. It is most commonly discussed in financial terms in relation to accounting and is a process that businesses go through at least once a year to ensure best practice in what they are doing.

A self-audit is a variation on the above theme, but this time involving you assessing and getting to know yourself. What *you* want. What *you* like. What is important to *you*. What *your* main aims are for the coming year. Presumably, before you made the commitment to your spouse, you did this sort of activity – though you may not have given it a name. When you decided that this person was right for you and that you would agree to their proposal – you had probably already analysed (or audited) how your individual personalities fit together, whether your values matched, whether you could encourage and support each other's goals – while ensuring that what you wanted as individuals could effectively combine into a joint life.

Make sense? If it's starting to, but you still need a bit more convincing, this example may better illustrate my point. Do you remember the 1988 Eddie Murphy film *Coming to America*? To this day, that film has some of the most memorable lines, and none more so than this exchange between Prince Akeem (the Eddie Murphy character) and Imani Izzi, a woman who had been promised to him since birth:

Imani Izzi:	*Ever since I was born, I have been trained to serve you.*
Prince Akeem:	*I know, but I'd like to know about you. What do you like to do?*
Imani Izzi:	*Whatever you like.*
Prince Akeem:	*What kind of music do you like?*
Imani Izzi:	*Whatever kind of music you like.*
Prince Akeem:	*I know what I like, and you know what I like, 'cause you were trained to know but I would like to know what you like. Do you have a favourite food?*
Imani Izzi:	*Yes.*
Prince Akeem:	*Good! What is your favourite food?*
Imani Izzi:	*Whatever you like!*
Prince Akeem:	*This is impossible. I command you not to obey me.*
Imani Izzi:	*No.*

Make sense now? Remember, the self-audit is not about you discounting what your other half wants. Far from it. Instead, the process of taking the time to refresh your memory about what you like and enjoy will help make you an even better partner – and one who has so many exciting things to work for that the post-wedding blues won't hit too hard.

Hello... my name is...

Whether you are now referred to as a Mrs or a Ms – an integral part of your post-wedding self-audit process is to get to know yourself again. In fact, it may even be worth getting reacquainted with yourself in more depth than before.

At my hen do (also known as a bachelorette party), my chief bridesmaid organised a bridal shower as part of the proceedings. It was awesome. It involved about twenty of my girlies (including my mum and aunt) sitting around in her living room – enjoying lots of nibbles and company from friends made throughout the years. There were also a series of games, including one where R and I were both asked a series of questions to see how well we knew each other.

I must admit, the scores weren't great – but I totally denied the joking allegations that we didn't know each other as well as we should, mainly because in that context, I felt I didn't know *myself* as well as I should.

Think about it. When you were a child, you had a favourite colour, animal, stuffed toy, book, subject at school... these were often the hot topics at school. In general, though, grown-up conversations don't really focus on favourites.

This became pretty clear at my bridal shower. Seriously, I struggled to come up with a single favourite book as there are so many I have loved. Next was favourite film... Could it still be *Dirty Dancing* as it had been at the age of thirteen? The bottom line is that I myself didn't know – and that in itself has the potential to present a challenge both to the single and the married you.

Luckily, it's also very easily fixable, so inspired by the quiz I faced during my hen do, I encourage you to take a few minutes to answer the following questions about yourself.

Self-audit exercise 1:

Take a few minutes to think about the following questions:

- What is my favourite movie?
- What is my favourite song/album?
- What is my favourite type of meal?
- What hobbies do I have or what do I enjoy doing? (If stuck, consider your hobbies as a child.)
- What would be my ideal thing to do on a free weekend?
- If money wasn't an object, what countries would I like to visit?

While this is a useful exercise in its own right, you can go a step further and turn it into a Mr and Mrs game for you and your hubby.

To do this:

1. Give yourselves time to think about these and of course any other questions you'd like to throw into the mix.
2. Laugh at yourselves as you quiz each other.
3. Make a decision to take some form of action with this refreshed information you have about each other. Plan a day involving the cinema and a picnic, or indeed whatever emerged as the ideal thing to do on a free weekend. Likewise with going to a restaurant for your favourite type of meal. Reciprocate.

What's in a name?

> *"What's in a name? That which we call a rose*
> *By any other name would smell as sweet."*

William Shakespeare

According to Shakespeare, there really isn't much in a name – but ask any recently married or about-to-be married woman if they agree – and chances are they will say, with respect, that the bard was wrong on this one.

There is something in a name, as many women who have debated internally over what name they will use post-marriage will testify.

Think about it… major life changes have recently taken place. In fact, you may even still be in the process of getting used to your new name, and while you are proud to have taken your husband's name, this does have (potentially unconscious) implications regarding who you are.

As such, this can become a factor in the self-audit process.

Nicola, UK wedding blogger, social commentator and creator of Belle Noir Bride, a blog targeted at black British brides (www.bellenoirbride.co.uk) highlights how complicated this can be:

> *I am currently going under 3 aliases - I changed my name on certain things ie 2 bank accounts, and my driver's license to my married name. For blogging purposes I hyphenated my name, and for work I have kept my maiden name. I think I will change my name at work when I change jobs, but at the moment there*

doesn't seem any reason to do it, also I quite like my maiden name so I am a bit reluctant to let it go straight away!

Bianca, who runs a fashion wholesale business, also sees the name change process as one with multiple stages:

I didn't change my name for about a year! I made the excuse that I would wait for all my visas to expire. But it was just laziness. I have always wanted to take my husband's name. I think it is a nice tradition. Although, having gotten married so late (which is normal nowadays) – I was so used to being called Bianca Bawa. So I kept Bawa as a middle name. I discussed this with pretty much everyone that I met, to get their opinion. It is not traditional in India to keep your maiden name, but my parents were the ones pushing me to keep Bawa or double barrel it. In the end I decided to keep it as a middle name. It helps for business as well. So I am glad that I did. But I hardly use it and I am sure that I will drop it someday in the future.

Newlywed Lexi Couchman (known as Lexi Jarman in her career in media sales) also explains her thinking about whether she changed her name:

For personal things such as my passport, yes. For business, no. My name is my currency and I felt that changing to my married name and changing my role would leave me un-contactable. Changing my name personally was a choice that I made solely as a demonstrable commitment to our friends and family outside of my professional life.

Ida, a newlywed who has grown up in varying parts of the world and has now settled in California with her new hubby decided against changing her name:

> *"I like my Swedish name and I'm very proud of it. It means "maple-tree leaf" in Swedish, and I love how close to nature it is. Also, there's a history that my name carries – my family heritage and my life so far! Getting married doesn't change me, and neither should it change my name. It's a personal decision."*

Clearly, there is no right or wrong approach regarding names after getting married.

In my research for this book, I have come across a wide spectrum of opinion regarding name changes. I have spoken to brides who see changing their name as an essential symbolic part of being a family, those who need to take a while to warm up to the idea of a name change, those who keep one name for business purposes and one for their personal life, those who aren't especially fond of their new spouse's name and more… with all perspectives being perfectly valid.

Asking the question 'Does changing your name change your personality?' to a Twitter audience also solicited some firm opinions, with @DollsLikeYouLtd saying "Not at all – your name can never be the essence of you. You became you through nature, nurture, experience etc, not name." At the opposite end of the spectrum, @chelseablack noted, "Yes it does. Best you both double barrel or both keep your own names. There is no longer ownership."

The name changing debate clearly shows no sign of abating.

Elizabeth, a public relations professional who was born in San Francisco and is now based in London decided to change her name because:

I wanted to be easily identifiable as belonging to the same family. I do miss my maiden name as I spent more than 35 years living with it. But even though my husband offered to take my surname, it didn't feel right and I felt more comfortable being the one to take on a revised identify. It's probably because I also made the move from my home country to the UK, so could connect changing my surname to a UK version of me.

I too flirted with the idea with staying true to my maiden name for business reasons. However, as the final days and months approached, it was the desire to create an immediately recognisable joint unit that won out. Though (I must admit), had I had an extremely unusual surname – or had my husband been burdened with a particularly unappealing one – the debate may have raged on. So, while the name game may have more significance now than in the 17th century when Shakespeare wrote Romeo and Juliet, one thing is clear – the element of choice is essential.

Additionally, your sense of 'self' is just as relevant in any of these scenarios whether or not you take the plunge. And, as the next section will reveal, there are a number of factors for new brides to get accustomed to as they adapt to their married status.

Further Reading

If interested in reading an article on the topic of changing names, visit The Independent online to read Clare Dwyer Hogg's article entitled *"Should women trade in their surname when they get married?"*

http://www.independent.co.uk/life-style/love-sex/marriage/should-women-trade-in-their-surname-when-they-get-married-1717794.html

The Independent, 25 June 2009

Real bride reflection experiences

Julie Dawson, a UK-based bride who married for the first time aged 47, woke up one day to the fact that she was now part of a couple – something which she loved, yet it still hit her hard after her 2008 wedding. Describing life before her engagement, she indicates that she would rank her life satisfaction as being 8 out of 10:

I only say 8 because of my job. I had a lovely fiancé, the man of my dreams really, a great house and lovely friends. My job was seriously lacking in enjoyment for me that is why the lower figure or else it would have been a 10.

I haven't always wanted to get married. I always thought it would be lovely but never took it for granted. In fact before I got married I had decided that I

*was going to stay single. I was later in life marrying
and before I met my husband I was happy in my life.*

Julie notes that she is slightly older than the average
first time bride and highlights that meeting your life partner can happen at any age (which is good news for the
increasing number of women of all ages who fear that they
won't meet the man of their dreams). Julie shares the highs
and lows of her journey towards loving her married life:

*At first I didn't have a [post-wedding] slump but it
started about three or four months after the wedding. I
started to think what would be our next big milestone
as a couple. We were older, didn't want children, had
already just bought a fabulous house. I sort of mourned
not being able to strive for those things that younger
married couples did. I also started to really realise that
this was for ever! I knew it was but it really hit home. I
was not scared but just a little sad that just me and the
adventures I had alone were gone forever. I truly don't
mind and it lasted only a few months but it did have
an impact on my poor husband who could not understand how I felt.*

The impact of getting married shouldn't be underesti-
mated. The vows which bind couples together are wonderful
and should be celebrated. After all, this is the reason why
we go through all the trouble of organising spectacular
wedding celebrations which represent 'us' as a couple! And
yet, on the other side of the big event, this has the potential
to affect our self-perceptions. As Julie says:

*Not that I mind but I did feel that I had a responsibil-
ity to the other person in everything I did. Although I*

*loved being a couple sometimes I mourned my single-
dom… even though I had been in my relationship five
years before I married and was totally settled.*

And this is what brides must realise after their ceremony. Yes, in terms of moving forward as a couple, it's essential to have shared dreams, goals and plans – however it is just as important to pay homage to what makes you *you* – even after you have that ring on your finger.

Jessica Bolduc, a twenty-something newlywed based in New York City recognised the importance of 'me-time' soon after her wedding. One of her top tips for new brides is to:

*Make some time for yourself. Treat yourself to a mani-
cure, go shopping, or read a book in your local coffee
shop. My husband is going away for the day in a
couple of weeks. I am excited for my scheduled massage
and to just take time for myself!*

Sound strange? It isn't really. It just reiterates much of the discussion earlier in this chapter. In the past 12–24 months (on average) while planning this fantastic event, most of your decisions and focus were based on 'we'. Thinking as a unit is an excellent discipline to get into in creating your happily ever after and planning the future, but for the reasons described above, brides should then make a concerted effort to do some singular thinking. The post-wedding blues can strike early on after your big day, and while you are lucky enough to now have a partner for life – it takes you gaining your own perspective to get past this temporary slump.

Self-audit exercise 2:

While most of the self-audit process is a reflective one, I encourage brides to make one aesthetic change as well – you would be amazed how significant an impact that can have on your post-wedding self.

Why?

On your wedding day, you looked stunning... gorgeous... and you took your husband's breath away. You never felt more beautiful and you know your family and friends looked at you with love and support. Excellent, that's how it should be on your big day. But where do you go from there? I for one refused to concede to the idea that I peaked on my wedding day. I'd like to think I can still turn heads!

Author disclaimer: Please note, I am not suggesting an extreme physical transformation, but perhaps one of the following:

- Cut your hair or change your hair colour – in a noticeable way
- Add some new items to your wardrobe – which are a variation on your usual style
- Emphasise different features with your make up (if you normally wear dark lipstick, go nude and play up your eyes instead)
- Buy yourself a piece of statement jewellery.

For me, the aesthetic tweak was twofold:

1. Three days after I got married, I went to the salon and cut my hair shorter than it had ever been. Coupled with the highlights, I left with a completely different look and felt great. Like many brides, I'd been growing my hair for the wedding and it felt liberating and bold to go for a cut I had been contemplating for a while but not had the guts to try.

2. More subtle – but just as satisfying – I treated myself to a proper grown-up watch at the duty-free in Barbados when we were on our way home from our Guyana ceremony. Jokingly referred to to as my "Mrs Visram" watch, this whimsical purchase cost me approximately £110 and even today when I look at my wrist, I remember the significance of my first treat to myself as a married woman.

So what does all of this mean?

As per the experiences shared by Julie, Jessica and me – the journey into happy marriage is an incredibly exciting one. But it's important to remember that this fabulous newlywed stage is the time not only to embrace your new union but importantly, to *rediscover you*. You can start by using the varying audit exercises in this chapter, including the one here:

Self-audit exercise 3:

Embrace the many things you have to look forward to after your wedding by conducting this exercise which will help you decide where to start:

- What have I always wanted to do? (Include things on the list that you have always deemed impossible for one reason or another.)

  _____

  _____

- What are my values? Adventure? Dedication? Excellence? Courage? Fun? What are the things that make me me? (If this is a tough exercise at the moment… hold on for the values-focused chapter coming up.)

  _____

  _____

- What activities/opportunities did I turn down in the run up to the wedding due to needing to focus at the time? Look into doing some of them now.

  _____

  _____

- What can I do that I have not tried before? (Bellydancing classes? Learning mandarin? A cooking course?)

_____

_____

- When did I last get together with my girl-friends for dinner/drinks/a girlie sleepover? Is it time to schedule in the next one?!

_____

_____

Remember... doing stuff as a Mr and Mrs will happen alongside all of this. Your dinners out, evenings in, your determination to pick up a new sport that you can do together – but these are just some of the anchors you can use to reconnect with the 'you' in your new union. Going through this process doesn't detract from your new status as a married couple. But it does reiterate your commitment to yourself as half of the couple, and your commitment to continuing to be the woman he fell in love with, as well as his new partner in sickness, health, wealth and all that life is set to throw at you.

Chapter **3**

Aims & Goals: Be a Goal-Setting Queen

> *"If you don't know where you are going,*
> *you'll end up someplace else."*
> Yogi Berra

What do Thomas Jefferson, Barack Obama, Richard Branson, Jay Sean, Aishwarya Rai, Queen Latifah and Tony Robbins have in common? Apart from being well-known public figures, it is reported that they have all acknowledged their belief in the power of goal setting in achieving success.

I imagine you have a similar belief – that goal setting is an important step towards creating success. Why would I say that without knowing you? Well... there are a few clues:

- You have picked up this book, a coaching book on post-wedding motivation – a clear indication that there is something you are looking to achieve and that you are committed to exploring the best way to do it.

- You are likely to have been recently married, are about to get married or are considering marriage. This is an institution kicked off by a wedding which usually involves some level of goal setting and motivation to organise. You may have already spotted that coaching is a useful tool. Or, you may be in the early stages of getting to know more, but you are certainly open to exploring new ways to help you achieve your aims.

- For those of you who are already married and held a fabulous celebration to mark the beginning of your journey, arranging this celebration would have been your goal for the last umpteen months. It yielded success and now you are ready to establish what your next goals may be. Perhaps you realise that without making a concerted effort to set some clear goals, you're in danger of feeling unfulfilled – even with a fabulous partner by your side.

No matter what industry you work in or what experience you have had to date, reading this far into this book indicates you have a level of appreciation for planning and the linked concept of goal setting. By the time you finish this chapter, this will be even more pronounced and by the end of this chapter, you will know more about:

- Common goal-setting occasions
- Creating SMART goals – information about effective goal setting
- Goal-setting tips for newlyweds
- Exercises to help your newlywed goal-setting process
- Creating the next best day of your life (i.e., understanding the many things to look forward to as a newlywed)
- What entrepreneurs and celebrities have said about goal setting

- How effective goal setting will be an integral ingredient in shifting from the post-wedding blues to the productive and motivated post-wedding state
- Beyond SMART: Goal-setting theory and some other approaches
- Don't go it alone: enlist the help of a coach.

Common goal-setting occasions

"Nothing can stop the man with the right mental attitude from achieving his goal; nothing on earth can help the man with the wrong mental attitude."

Thomas Jefferson

Have you ever set a goal?

Having always been what I would describe as a 'driven' person, the concept of setting and having goals was one that I had grown-up with. But it was only as an adult that I properly learned and researched further into the most effective ways to set goals.

What is a goal?

According to the Merriam Webster dictionary, a goal is defined as "the end toward which effort is directed." Essentially, it is an aim you have for yourself.

Through your life, this may have included areas of your life in anything from getting 10 out of 10 in a spelling test to convincing you parents that you really do deserve that dolls playhouse for Christmas. Later in life, this might be achieving success in a university degree, buying a house, paying off your student debts, saving enough money to buy a car, starting your own business, becoming slimmer, gaining a promotion and so much more.

Whether or not you consider yourself to be a committed goal setter, chances are you have made some attempts along the way.

"Deciding to commit yourself to long term results,
rather than short term fixes, is as important as any
decision you'll make in your lifetime."

Tony Robbins

On birthdays, when you blow out the candles on your cake, it's traditional to make a wish. This wish can often be indicative of something you are striving for – unless it's a pure genie in a bottle wish like wishing Will Smith was there to celebrate with you! Exceptions like that aside, those wishes are a great clue to something which you could effectively turn into a goal.

Even more commonly, once a year, it seems like the whole world undergoes the process together – the time when we all set New Year resolutions. This is a process that we can all relate to. You know the drill. It's dark, cold and potentially snowy outside (unless you are lucky enough to live somewhere in the Caribbean, Africa, Asia or Australia). Christmas day came and went with the usual excitement of a fantastic spread, lots of presents and family time. Festive cheer remains in the air, but what next? Apart from feeling that you cannot eat another bite and the enjoyment of playing with any new toys you gained as presents, the next step tends to be looking towards the next year.

This takes two forms, a very short-term view and what should ideally be a much longer-term one. The former is what to do for New Year's Eve and the latter is what your New Year resolutions are likely to be.

I sense some dissent in the ranks. What's that you say? I'm wrong? You don't make New Year resolutions? Don't even think about it? Don't believe in them? They only lead to disappointment? Waste of time you say?

What makes some of you say that? Might you be someone who wears your 'New Year Resolution sceptic' badge with pride?

If that's the case, you are certainly not the only one that applies to and that notion leads me nicely on to my next point. While I wholeheartedly believe that we generally have aims and goals in terms of what we want to achieve, not many of us set goals effectively.

A guide to effective goal setting

Q: What is the difference between a dream and a goal?
A: A piece of paper

There are a number of factors that inform how effective or otherwise a goal is, with some golden rules to follow to make sure you are placing yourself in the best possible position to be successful.

Golden Rules:
- Make your goals SMART (Specific, Measurable, Attainable, Relevant and Time Phased).
- Write down your goals. This is key. There are many different definitions of what a goal is versus

a dream but for me the answer "a piece of paper" is a favourite.

- State your goals in the positive. It's *much* more powerful to set a goal to gain a 2.1 in your undergraduate degree than to set a goal not to fail. It is common to state that we want to lose weight as opposed to wanting to become slimmer or healthier. Frame positively.

- Share your goals... don't just keep them to yourself. Talking to others about your aspirations and goals helps to make them real. It's almost a step beyond writing them down on paper because when you share personal goal information with a partner, family member, friend, acquaintance or even your Facebook and Twitter networks – suddenly it adds an element of accountability as you'll find people start asking you about how you are getting on with achieving it.

- Work with a coach. If you really are serious about effective goal setting, this is an important rule for you. Coaching is a process where you work (usually one-on-one) with a qualified coach who is able to help you achieve your goals faster than you would be able to on your own. Through a series of (often) bi-weekly sessions, the clarity of working with a coach becomes clear as you will be questioned, challenged, prompted, pushed and more into creating not only clear goals for yourself but also ones that will push you beyond your comfort zone in a positive way.

- Take consistent action. Every successful entrepreneur and business person I have encountered talks about not just taking singular actions but being consistent. Always do something to move yourself forward and closer to the goal. The notion I always remember highlights that knowledge is not power, consistent action is.
- Any goal you set yourself should fit in the realm of something that is firmly within your control. It is amazing how many people waste effort engaging in something that is essentially goal setting for others.

Goal setting with a real formula and purpose can be incredibly powerful – however without following the rules above, you risk that common New Year's fatigue – the feeling that sometimes comes from not succeeding in an aim you have… again.

Make your goals SMART

> *"Without a specific goal there can be endless drifting, a floating on the winds of this good idea and then that one."*

Laura Whitworth, Karen Kimsey-House *et al*,
Co-Active Coaching

Goal setting gives you a specific direction and action plan for making something real. SMART goal setting is an integral part of that process, and involves being:

- **S**pecific
- **M**easurable
- **A**ttainable
- **R**elevant
- **T**ime-phased.

Specific

Establishing a clear goal-setting process can make a big difference in your success. The Co-Active Coaching team emphasise that:

> *The best goals are specific. They are action orientated... for example, the goal "think about moving to Alaska" will be strengthened by action including buying a book about Alaska, [writing in a] journal her memories of Alaska – and this is even further enhanced by a schedule.*

A bit closer to home, it becomes clear that being specific is key, no matter what the aim. See below for some specific versus non-specific goals:

Non-specific goals	Specific goals
My goal is to do well in my degree.	My goal is to achieve a 2.1 (upper second) or above within three years.
My goal is to expand my networks.	Each month I will add fifteen new LinkedIn contacts and attend one live networking event.
My goal is to save money.	I will save a minimum of £2,400 this year, by saving at least £200 a month.

For most of us who are seeking to achieve something (anything), this is a great skill to develop. Even in wedding planning, the goal "to make sure I delegate" is far inferior to a goal to "delegate organising the flowers and buying the wine to two bridesmaids X and Y". It is being specific that results in powerful goals with a greater chance of a successful result.

There is no room to be vague in effective goal setting. You should make your goal as detailed as you can envisage it, so you know and can almost touch / feel what you are trying to achieve.

Measurable

> *"There is no happiness except in the realization that we have accomplished something."*

Henry Ford

The measurable aspect of SMART goal setting is the key to happiness. That's right… the key to happiness. It really is.

This is because without measure, you actually cannot tell/will not know when you have achieved your goal. This is often evident in those stories you hear about lottery winners who always had a dream of winning the lottery but soon after winning, become bankrupt and become depressed. This, despite the fact that they achieved their dream of achieving mass wealth – at levels that the rest of us can often only dream of. What happens in these instances is that winners may have been specific about what they want (a new house, a round the world trip), but they haven't necessarily given themselves the space to measure what happiness or success really means to them. Therefore, even with vast amounts of material things, they may end up feeling empty and unable to celebrate their success due to missing this part of the goal-setting process.

This is also true when it comes to the goals you set for your marriage. While a goal to have a happy marriage makes absolute sense on the surface – if you are unable to measure what 'happy' means to you personally and you as a couple, you are setting yourself up for unhappiness. However, if you agree that a happy marriage for you will ideally involve eating together at least three times a week, having a constant stream of communication, being honest and faithful, not taking each other for granted, respecting each other's aspirations and having a mutual support system – then you are in a better position to measure your success. For some couples, a happy marriage may also consist of extending the union by having children. Ultimately while different individuals and couples will have varied definitions, it's important that your goals are measurable so you are better equipped to know whether you are at the level you want, or if you are below or above the aim.

Attainable

> *"It is better to fall short of a high mark*
> *than to reach a low one."*
>
> H. C. Payne

What was the last goal you set which you achieved successfully? Do you have any goals which remain on your to-do list?

If you've ever been shocked by the heights of what someone can achieve, you may already realise that if you carefully craft a plan of action to achieve your goals, the seemingly impossible may become possible, if you take it step by step.

Whether a goal is attainable or not is based on a combination of what is realistic and a reflection of your mental attitude and level of determination towards a task.

Maintain a level of realism and recognise that it is important that you don't dismiss particular aspirations you have as being unattainable, just because that voice in your head says *you can't* or *it's silly* or *it's above your abilities*. There's a fine line between realising what is attainable and allowing the voices in your head to tell you that you're not capable of something.

If you don't quite understand the difference between which goals are challenging in a positive way and which are unattainable in a detrimental way, then take this example (it's a personal one that you may relate to).

If I set a goal to run a marathon within a month, this would be unattainable for me. Long-distance running has never ever been my forte (even when growing up in Kenya and cross country was imposed on us). However, please note that I am not saying I could never run a marathon. Instead, the unattainable aspect of that goal is the timeframe. As running five kilometres is something I currently find challenging, the aim of running a marathon within a month is not realistic for me. However, a more attainable goal for me would be to train to successfully run five kilometres within a month, for example. Forgive me if that approach sounds obvious, but my experience in personal development coaching has shown me that it's often neglecting to turn a large goal into bite-sized chunks that makes it seem out of reach.

With that in mind, here's another example to emphasise why the attainable aspect of goal setting is important. As a bride who shared her wedding date with Kate Middleton and Prince William, I could have said that "My goal is for our wedding to rival the royal wedding" but that would have had some fundamental flaws. Of course, it's easy to spot the issues with that particular goal.

1. Without advance information about the plans for the royal wedding, there was no advance benchmark to compare the two weddings.

2. There are no specifics detailed in this goal. What exactly is to be rivalled? The size of the venue? The quality of the food? The number of guests? How raucous the dancing became?

3. And oh yes, how *could* I forget… the fact that financially, the two couples involved were on *such* different financial footing that a comparison of this nature was not only unattainable, but was also ludicrous.

Attainable: effective goal setting tips

Remember, deciding whether or not your goal is attainable is potentially a tricky part of the process, often due to the fact that the doubting voices in your head can wreak havoc on your attempt to make an informed decision about whether or not something is attainable.

In evaluating your goal, remember that whether or not something is attainable often goes hand in hand with the timing you place on achieving said goal. While Richard Branson has built an admirable empire over a number of decades, he did not achieve it overnight. He took some knocks along the way and persevered with his aims.

In thinking about a specific goal, ask yourself:

- What resources do I have at my disposal to help me achieve it?
- Which part of my networks can I tap into to make this goal more attainable?
- Who do I know who has successfully achieved what I am trying to and what can I learn from them?
- What direct research conversations can I have that would provide additional insight to hours of internet searching?
- Who can I partner with to make goal success more likely?
- And when in doubt ask yourself:
- Who says I can't do it/this isn't attainable?

If the answer is *you* and it is for a reason other than too tight a time frame, keep your head up, ignore that voice… and keep striving!

Relevant

"We want to set the goals that our heart conceives, that our mind believes and that our bodies will carry out."

It is in the process of goal setting and truly establishing what it is you want to achieve, that you start to decide what is relevant to you. A dream or goal you had as a child or even as an adult a few years ago may not still be relevant to your current aspirations. This is an important thing to establish before you start being down on yourself about not achieving success in something that you may not have realised is no longer relevant to you.

Until my late teenage years, my dream was – and had always been – to become a foreign correspondent. I grew up in Kenya watching *CNN International* daily, and at the time, my dad worked for the United Nations in countries including Sudan, Somalia, Rwanda and more – and I was absolutely fascinated with international relations. My love of writing and media made journalism the obvious career aspiration for me. I worked towards it diligently and I wrote for any school media we had. At the age of 15 (when still based in Kenya) I was published in an international anthology of global student articles and offered an undergraduate place to study journalism at Emerson College in Boston. And the love affair continued throughout my university years. When studying Politics, International Studies and Gender at Warwick University, I became a fixture on student station *RaW (Radio Warwick)*. I even went on to complete (with distinction, I am proud to say), a master's degree in International Journalism at Cardiff University.

Am I proud of these accomplishments? Absolutely. Did I fulfil my goal of achieving a good undergraduate and postgraduate degree? Quite successfully I'd say. Did I go on to be an award-winning journalist reporting on the front line of some of the world's most memorable conflicts, like my idol Christiane Amanpour? That I did not.

Why?

Well… somewhere along the line, my values, interests and priorities shifted; therefore, my goals should have as well. I had made a practical financial decision that an entry-level journalist salary wouldn't suffice for a girl needing to pay rent and support herself in London – so what did I do? Did I move to South America to live with my parents and pursue the dream there? I did not. Instead, I continued my life in the UK, sticking as close to journalism and journalists as I could without actually being one. I worked for Pearson plc (owner of *The Financial Times*, Penguin books and Pearson Education), the business and finance channel *CNBC* and global news channel *BBC World*, all in communications/PR positions – before ending up at a broadcast public relations consultancy for three and a half years.

It was sometime between the university achievements and one of my earlier roles at these media organisations that I allowed myself to recognise and evaluate the relevance of the goals I was setting.

What I realised, when I gave myself the opportunity, is that I had been on the periphery of that childhood goal for so long, even after I consciously varied my career route. And yet I had never taken the time to properly acknowledge to myself that I no longer wanted to be a foreign correspondent. It seems that my goals to report on the world's conflicts had turned into something more – dare I say – safe. While there is absolutely nothing wrong with that, I could have avoided a number of instances of disappointment in myself along the years if I had taken stock of which of my goals were still relevant.

Interestingly, my dad alluded to this shift during his speech at our wedding – telling the throng of 180 guests about how it took him a while to figure out why his driven daughter was not being receptive to his leads when it came to journalistic jobs in the Caribbean, in the States and in East Africa. While I always politely thanked him for sending me on the information, I never outright said that my international journalism goal had metamorphosed. It felt strange to admit that the globally raised, academically capable, much travelled, ambitious teenager had turned into a woman who had career goals firmly stuck in rainy London, as opposed to a far flung exotic destination.

What my dad respectfully acknowledged at our wedding, was that while I was still working towards my own goals, there had been a shift in balance as individual dreams had become our dreams.

Time phased

"There's still plenty to do. I think I'll never run out of things to accomplish, as long as I'm alive, because there's so much to learn, and so much to do. I always feel like I have so much further to go, personally, spiritually, emotionally, mentally, and physically."

Queen Latifah

What is the deadline for achieving your goal?

This line of questioning can often make the most ambitious of us squirm. But the time-phased element of goal setting is integral if we are to set effective action-orientated goals. If you were to have the SMAR aspects of your goals, without the T – it would mean that you are not pushing yourself to make things happen as soon as they could.

If we didn't make our goals time specific, it is likely that we would procrastinate in a major way. After all, what would be the impetus to achieve this goal? If it's completely open-ended, you would feel like you can work on it at any time.

Would this approach challenge us? Make us work at our best? Definitely not.

Interestingly, in wedding planning, we are often at our most disciplined when it comes to ensuring our goals are time phased – because they have to be! Planning a wedding is the ultimate motivator because, unless you move the wedding date, you have one pre-determined goal deadline – and lots of smaller goal deadlines to build up to the big day. If you don't order your flowers by a certain date, you'll have none. If you don't set a time-specific goal for buying your dress and shoes, sending your invitations or even for purchasing your travel tickets for your honeymoon, none of those significant aspects of the getting married process will happen in the way you want them to.

Essentially, if life was infinite – we would not have the urgency needed to make things happen. One of the golden rules of goal setting is that your goal should be challenging – stretch you beyond your comfort zone to motivate you to work hard to achieve your best. Ensuring your goals are time phased is an integral aspect in this process.

A succinct reflection on this comes from Apple visionary, the late Steve Jobs:

> *Your time is limited. Don't waste it living someone else's life. Don't be trapped by dogma, which is living the result of other people's thinking. Don't let the noise of others' opinions drown your own inner voice. And, most important, have the courage to follow your heart and intuition. They somehow already know what you truly want to become.*

Time-phased: quick time-setting exercise

When it comes to deciding on the deadline you are going to give yourself for achieving your goal, it is important that you strike the right balance.

Don't give yourself so much time that the goal isn't a challenge, yet don't give yourself such a short period of time that you suffer anxiety and stress in the process.

To find your middle ground, you just need to say your SMAR goal out loud a few times with varying times at the end of your sentence (by September, by December, within the next two years etc)

Once you stumble across a time that doesn't make you break into cold sweats, but makes you realise you need to get your skates on and organise yourself pronto, you have found the right time period for that goal.

Goal setting tips for newlyweds: creating more 'best' days of your life

> *"How am I going to live today in order to create the tomorrow I'm committed to?"*
>
> Tony Robbins

Goal setting for newlyweds luckily follows all of the same rules as per the above. So once you embrace these golden rules, you will be well placed to make some solid goals of your own.

However… if you believe that your wedding day was and will always be the definitive best day of your life – you are doing yourself a disservice as you have so much to offer as an individual and as a couple!

Please be aware that always referring to your wedding day as the best day of your life implies that there is nowhere to go but down. This is surely the most inappropriate attitude with which to begin a marriage. Your spouse is not the consolation prize from your fabulous wedding day… s/he is the reward earned from the relationship to date and your commitment to the future and each other. Your day was a magical, never to be forgotten event where, as a couple, you officially vowed to commit to and support each other. But you are now at your launching pad – not your landing pad. Instead of coming back down to earth with a thud, effective goal setting will mean that you do the opposite – take off like a rocket.

Real bride goal-setting experience

> *"Goals are the fuel in the furnace of achievement."*
>
> Brian Tracy, Eat that Frog

London-based newlywed Nicola describes what she enjoyed in the planning process of her wedding:

> *I absolutely loved planning the wedding and revelled over every decision that needed to be made. I used it to spend quality time with my Mum, as during the process I did a lot of dress shopping and wedding fairs and I did this all with her. I would do lots of research and then shortlist the options which I then presented to Ashley for his thoughts. I was pretty relaxed throughout the process, and then naturally got stressed about 2 weeks beforehand.*

Whether or not she was doing this in a concerted way, chances are, Nicola is an effective goal setter if she managed to achieve so much and keep stress at bay until the last few weeks. But she'd also set her sight her sights on something that she didn't really have any control over:

> *I thought I was going to have a honeymoon baby!?! When it didn't happen I felt really down. So I knew that I needed a project to occupy my mind. I had the idea for the blog about 3 months into my planning, so decided to throw myself into working on it.*

Nicola says that in the days and weeks following her beautiful wedding and honeymoon, she *"felt a bit lost initially, I suddenly had lots of free time on my hands."* In these moments after the wedding excitement, Nicola's hope for a honeymoon baby was something that she didn't have complete control over. As mentioned in the chapter, this can often lead to disappointment (generally and in yourself) even though it really isn't something within your control.

Manchester-based bride Salma Alam-Naylor acknowledges that her situation before her wedding meant that after it, she had set herself some major goals.

Before Salma's engagement, she was very dissatisfied with her life because she was unhappy in her job. She explains that before she got engaged she was trying to make something of her music career. She notes:

Despite being blissfully happy with my now-husband at the time, I was also suffering from some health problems (which have gladly subsided), and was quite overweight at the time (too many date nights in with Richard!) which didn't help in my general feeling good, and was facing a lot of prejudice about my relationship with Richard from his friends. A picture of happiness! ;)

This was all set to change after the wedding however as this driven bride had no intention of letting an unsatisfied feeling fester. After the new couple's return from honeymoon, the bride quickly took some further steps towards her goal:

I went successfully through the interview process for my teacher training course. I felt like I'd started a new chapter in my life and I felt liberated and excited that I was finally making something of a career!

Newlywed Stacy Moore felt the pressure to set some serious goals as soon as her honeymoon was over. Stacy was an educational psychologist who worked with young people via educational establishments. She had very recently taken redundancy and gone from full-time salaried employment to being self-employed. Her summer wedding and honeymoon meant time was of the essence regarding what she needed to achieve professionally:

> *I began to feel anxious about the upcoming school summer holidays as I knew that during this time I would not be earning and this caused me a great deal of anxiety. I became more worried about being self-employed and felt more responsible for ensuring the bills were paid.*

For Stacy, the most significant thing that she did on return from honeymoon was pitching for some new business for her fledgling consultancy:

> *I went to pitch my new business to an inclusion manager at a Further Education college. I felt weirdly 'grown-up' in doing this and it felt good to 'get back out there' following such an amazing period in my life. Straight after that I had another meeting discussing my business with another college and I began feeling very nervous about the implications of these meetings. If I didn't secure work it wasn't just me that would suffer, it would be my husband too. This was a sobering feeling.*

From planning a family to going self-employed and starting a new job to starting a blog – it is clear that there is no shortage of potential goals for a new bride.

Newlywed Nicola's advice is to *"Have a project – have something that you can focus on, utilising that free time you suddenly have will make you feel positive when you might be feeling down."*

Married within the last few years, Julie Dawson shares

words of wisdom with newlyweds who are readjusting to life after their wedding day. She says *"Enjoy your free time from wedding planning. Use the extra time to put into your relationship or career or both."*

Sound advice indeed, and even more will be explored in Chapter 8.

Enlist the support of a coach

The authors of *Co-Active Coaching* explain it well when they say:

> *The most visible outcome of coaching is also the primary reason clients want coaching in the first place: action. Coaching clients want change. They want to see results. They want to move forward. It is for exactly this reason that one of the recommended processes in effective goal setting is enlisting the support of a qualified coach...*

> *Coaching is a useful vehicle for quality goal setting because, as described in Co-Active Coaching, within the container of the coaching relationship, coach and client work together on the client's behalf. Clients bring an agenda for change. They bring desire and a host of qualities that include willingness to dive in, commitment to their lives and education to their own purpose.*

In a move from wishes and intentions – a major benefit of working with a coach is their expertise in splitting a goal into manageable pieces.

How to kick your own butt – be your own coach:

Until you get your own coach (or if you are between coaching sessions), ask yourself these questions if you feel your enthusiasm for working towards your goal waning:

- How can I make the process more fun when I get frustrated?
- What am I willing to sacrifice to give the achievement of this goal the attention it deserves?
- How will I feel when I have achieved my goal?
- How will I feel if I don't achieve this goal?

Goal-setting theory and approaches beyond SMART:

SMART goal setting, as described above, represents a common way to structure goals and is one that I highly recommend. However, once you have mastered this approach, there are additional elements worth exploring.

Goal-setting theory

The website, mindtools.com, published an article highlighting that in the late 1960s, Dr Edwin Locke led some pioneering research on goal setting and motivation. His research showed that there was a relationship between how difficult and specific a goal was and people's performance of a task. He found that specific and difficult goals led to better task performance than vague or easy goals.

Similar to earlier descriptions in the 'specific' section of this chapter, he notes that telling someone to "Try hard" or "Do your best" is less effective than "Try to get more than 80% correct" or "Concentrate on beating your best time." Likewise, having a goal that's too easy is not a motivating force. Hard goals are more motivating than easy goals, because it's much more of an accomplishment to achieve something that you have to work for.

Furthermore, in 1990, Edwin Locke (along with Gary Latham), published a seminal work, *A Theory of Goal Setting and Task Performance.* In this book, they reinforced the need to set specific and difficult goals. Although this study was based on organisational and work-based goal setting, a couple of elements are relevant for post-wedding motivation goal setting so I have included the relevant aspects below.

Clarity: Clear goals are measurable and unambiguous. When a goal is clear and specific, with a definite time set for completion, there is less misunderstanding. When a goal is vague – or when it's expressed as a general instruction, like "take the initiative" – it has limited motivational value.

The article reiterates that "When you use the SMART acronym to help you set goals, you ensure the *clarity* of the goal by making it Specific, Measurable and Time-bound."

Challenge: One of the most important characteristics of goals is the level of challenge. We are often motivated by achievement, and are therefore likely to judge a goal based on the significance of the anticipated accomplishment. When you know that what you do will be well received (for example by an audience if you are starting a blog, or by brides if setting up a flower or cake business), there's a natural motivation to do a good job. When setting goals, you should make each goal a challenge. If the post-wedding goal or project you have set yourself is easy or not very important – and if you don't expect the accomplishment to be significant – then the effort may not be impressive.

As described earlier in this chapter and again with this reminder from mindtools.com, it's important to strike an appropriate balance between a challenging goal and an attainable goal. "Setting a goal that you'll fail to achieve is possibly more demotivating than setting a goal that's too easy. The need for success and achievement is strong, therefore people are best motivated by challenging, but realistic, goals." Remember this in your post-wedding goal setting.

Goal-setting coaching exercise: the rocking chair test

This is my favourite goal-setting exercise, and it never fails to work with any of my clients – including young people who sometimes don't engage with the concept of goal setting:

Imagine that you are 85 years old and sitting in a rocking chair on a porch or balcony. Next to you is an inquisitive young person who asks you what you would consider to be the biggest accomplishments in your life. What are you most proud of? Tell them. (Say them out loud and write them down in the process.)

Exercises to inspire your newlywed goal setting process

Goal-setting worksheet for newlyweds

Name _____ Date: _____

As an individual, what will be my biggest achievement in the next year?

_____

_____

_____

As a couple, what will be our biggest achievement in the next year?

_____

_____

_____

How can we encourage each other on the journey to achieving these goals?

_____

_____

_____

Whenever I feel deflated about this process, I need to remember that…

_____

_____

What would we like to be celebrating/which achievements will be looking back at proudly in 5–10 years' time?

_____

_____

Chapter 4

People Power: Re-establish your networks

"The richest people in the world look for and build networks, everyone else looks for work."

Robert Kiyosaki

When you think about your network of contacts, what groups in your life come to mind? Your Facebook contacts? Your family? Maybe the people you have on LinkedIn, or the group of friends you grew up with?

According to the Merriam Webster dictionary, networking is the "exchange of information or services among individuals, groups, or institutions; *specifically*: the cultivation of productive relationships for employment or business."

This is useful, but we are thinking in the broadest sense of the word. In this day and age, the word network generally goes hand in hand with your professional life and is closely linked with the word social. Your network on any level is likely to include friends, family, current work colleagues, ex-colleagues, university acquaintances, and contacts you know through any activities you do and committees you are part of.

Another definition, courtesy of Dictionary.com, refers to networking as "a supportive system of sharing information and services among individuals and groups having a common interest". This is the definition I will lean towards when talking about the personal aspect of networking. This is really more about connection in general. It doesn't tend to be as strategic as business networking but is more about creating the connections we need for our own wellbeing and happiness.

When you are in the throes of planning your wedding, it is sometimes hard to maintain these networks and the months following your wedding are an excellent time to really assess your network, ensuring it is working for you in the best way possible.

In this chapter, you will learn the importance of reconnecting with your networks, and in getting past any post-wedding disconnection feelings you may have.

Why is it important to focus on my networks?

"Call it a clan, call it a network, call it a tribe,
call it a family: Whatever you call it,
whoever you are, you need one."

Jane Howard

What do your networks have to do with regaining your post wedding productivity? How will re-establishing your networks have an impact on your return to non-wedding planning life?

When we think of networks and modern day networking, there is sometimes an impression of the superficial. However, re-establishing, reconnecting and embracing our networks are an integral part in the path towards motivation and productivity in our lives and careers after we get married.

Defined as an interconnected group or system these days, your active networks are a reflection on the current stage of your life. As such, updating your networks is an integral part of getting back on track after your wedding extravaganza.

You may be thinking that while you have a close group of friends, you may not particularly have many networks, please let me prove you wrong. Remember networks can include:

- Your family
- Your school friends
- Your university friends
- School and university acquaintances (people who were involved with the same society or course that you were)
- Ex-colleagues
- Current colleagues
- Friends of friends
- Contacts and connections made via Twitter, LinkedIn and more
- Your spouse

Still believe networking and re-establishing connections isn't significant? I hope not.

While networking may not be the word you would use to describe calling a few girlfriends and planning a movie night, the fact that our networks consist of all of the people we choose to have within our close and extended circles means that it is important to pay attention to these groups in order to feel more fulfilled. On a personal level, you can think of them as connections if that feels more appropriate to you.

Remember, while you have said "I do" to one person, it is still your immediate group of friends or family who will contribute to fulfilling your wider sense of being. Some parts of our networks may be very significant to regaining our purpose, routine and post-wedding excitement after the big day.

Now that you appreciate the basis of networking and its significance, the rest of this chapter will highlight what steps you can take to regain/strengthen this aspect of your life and highlight the benefits of doing so. At the same time, reminding you that the most significant new part of your daily network is your spouse.

We will look at:

- Networking: personal (connection with friends *and* your spouse)
- Networking: professional
- Networking: social

Networking: personal

> *"A good friend is a connection to life – a tie to the past, a road to the future, the key to sanity in a totally insane world."*

Lois Wyse

Reconnect with friends

While I enjoyed being around my girlfriends/bridesmaids frequently – especially in the months leading up to the wedding – it was in the months immediately afterwards that I realised I had missed *a lot* when it came to what was going on in their lives.

How could that have happened? Quite easily it

seems. Despite my efforts not to be a 'me me me' bride, I invariably missed some going out occasions with my girls, therefore was not in the loop. During my fifteen months of planning and preparation, I had missed brunches, weekend dinners and clubbing nights out – all of which meant that I was not up to date on the most recent goings on.

More than that, I realised some of my friends had deliberately opted out of calling me regularly for a catch up because they did not want to distract/bother me!

Crazy right? I thought so, but it seems that friends sometimes think they are being considerate to their bride-to-be friends by not 'burdening' them with additional information about what is going on in their lives.

Very soon after our wedding, it became clear to me that even for brides who are not especially self-absorbed, you miss out on events due to the responses of those around you. That said, there's a chance that even if I was physically present for some conversations, I did not necessarily absorb the details of the topic being discussed. But in the main, my lack of being in touch was simply due to not being around on as regular a basis.

What was your experience with your friends?

London bride Lexi Couchman made sure her networks remained strong. *"As a couple, and as individuals, we have always worked hard to remain close with those that are important to us."*

Jeannine Archer Duhaney found that the challenge in re-establishing these networks lay in balancing her priorities. *"My network of friends and family were not difficult to reconnect with after marriage. Work is what made that difficult. I was working so many hours that I allowed myself to lose touch."*

Bianca Bawa Skinner, who travels a lot due to her fashion wholesale business notes *"Because I travel so much, it is really hard to juggle meeting up with friends and spending enough time with my husband. Often I want to just stay at home and be with him when I am in town, but we both know it's important for me to meet the girls as often as I can."*

New York based bride Jessica Bolduc shares her experience:

> *The wedding planning process was a mix of things – fun, stressful and bittersweet. I loved the days when my bridesmaids, my mom and I would get together, have lunch, and talk wedding plans. I really enjoyed spending that special time with them and discussing all of the little details that make the big day come together. I am not a girl who is that patient with arts and crafts, so the DIY projects like my favours and programs ended up stressing me out more than they should.*

It seems her experience was similar to what I have described. A very special, unique and memorable time of connecting with family and close girl friends on one level – yet the topic of conversation at these moments was often the big day. Entirely appropriate of course, but this makes it easier and easier to see how time spent together may not necessarily equate with being up to date on the latest goings on with the members of this close-knit group.

London-based bride Stacy Moore even noted that one of the tough things after getting married has been *"getting back in touch with friends as I had been out of the loop for so long and therefore had limited things to talk about with them".*

Does the married/single divide between friends end up being a barrier? It's something Stacy is conscious of although the jury is out on whether this is a real challenge or not. Stacy says:

Meeting up with friends who aren't married has also been tough to some extent as I am aware of the possibility of their perceptions of me as being a newly 'smug-married'! A lot more of what I talk about now naturally involves my husband so it sometimes feels I might talk about him too much in conversations. But no one has ever said this – maybe I'm being overly sensitive!

So what is the next step?

The Solution...

Work hard to ensure that you do *not* become one of those people who lose contact with significant friends, family and others after your wedding.

The reason why you may not have been as present as you would have liked to be in the run up to your wedding is clear. However, the solution to being out of touch with these personal networks is similarly understandable. Make real efforts to get together and catch up. Yes, you may get together after the wedding to scrapbook or enjoy the photos/video – but the mission here is to create opportunities to get away from anything wedding related and focus on your friends and family.

What is going on in their lives? How are their relationships going? For singles – what has been the latest gossip/amusement on the dating scene? How has work been? What are they celebrating in their lives and what are their main challenges? How can you be there to listen, support and everything in between?

This will serve to strengthen those relationships. Remember, the ring on your finger represents a lifelong commitment to the person you have chosen – not an electric fence which keeps others out!

This is all part of the process of regaining and resetting the perspective and focus that was present during the planning time.

This chapter entirely advocates making time to really focus on your networks as a significant step in overcoming the post-wedding blues and regaining your post-wedding motivation.

As you settle into married life, it's an excellent time to ask w*hat is important to me, and why?*

When planning a wedding, everything seems so important, essential even. After all, how can we make sure everything is just-so if we don't pay attention to minute details? I consider myself to have been pretty laid back as far as brides go – really, I was. However, I can still remember the frustration bubbling up internally over the world's (well UK retailers') lack of understanding about what turquoise is. Not aqua. Not teal. Not sky blue – but turquoise. I wasn't uber-fussy about much, so was the correct colour too much to ask?! (Rant over.)

After the wedding, a key part of being open to reconnecting in the right ways is step off the 'it- has-to-be-just-so' accelerator a bit. Set your goals, establish your aspirations as mentioned in Chapter 3, but allow yourself some flexibility. Brides don't necessarily recognise the intense level of pressure they put on themselves when it comes to creating a perfect day. They may not realise that at this special time, the world – at least their world – really does revolve around them. After her wedding, bride Salma Alam-Naylor, recognised this and shared her learnings on a post-wedding blog on the English Weddings website - http://english-wedding.com/2011/05/on-the-other-side/ :

Blog theme: 'On the Other Side':

Yes, I am back! I am slightly nervous to be back. I don't know why. Perhaps it has to do with not wanting to accept it's all over – or perhaps because being 'on the other side' has changed my perspective about a lot of things, and caused me to realise I became quite a wedding monster during the run up to my wedding! I don't want to say 'Bridezilla' – because I'm a nice girl and I wasn't mean to anyone. I say wedding monster because I became greedy for validation. I wanted my wedding to be everywhere and I wanted everyone to know about it. I wanted my wedding to be featured on EVERY BLOG IN THE WORLD.

I totally missed the point. All that doesn't actually matter. When you spend hours looking at other weddings you want to envisage your wedding being celebrated and appreciated by the whole world in the same way. But I don't need that now. No one really needs that. I have my own memories. I have my own validation. I have the words from my friends and family that mean more to me than any stranger's words could ever mean. And more importantly – I have my husband.

I was scared to admit this at the time because I didn't think it had really happened to me. But it had. I was more obsessed with what the internet thought of me than what the people around me had to say. I do not regret becoming part of English Wedding and the wedding blogging world. But I do regret getting so wrapped up in its world that I at times neglected what was most important to me. To all of you beautiful friends I am sorry.

I've noticed I haven't gifted you with one of Salma's lessons in quite a while. Perhaps the most important lesson I have learnt is:

Remember what is truly important. You do not need to seek validation.

Salma's blog represents something which is not uncommon with brides. This is an example of how during the wedding process, not only do we sometimes end up being more out of touch with our friends and their lives than we would like to be, but also, we can slightly lose who we are.

Wedding blogs and online communities are prolific, and it can feel like joining a special club when you fit into this very proud, excitable community. Post-wedding, it becomes time to reassess what is truly important if we are to move towards the post-wedding motivation we crave.

Networking exercise 1:

These are by no means difficult tasks, but as life and busyness often get in the way, I have created a short list of tasks you should complete in order to begin the process of reconnecting with your personal networks.

Tick them off as you complete them – this may be the most enjoyable to do list ever!

1. Contact 3–4 of your closest girlfriends and propose an activity that will allow you to spend some quality time together. Good possibilities include booking a spa day, simultaneous nail appointments, an old fashioned sleepover etc. Inappropriate activities for this specific task include clubbing and cinema as they won't allow you the quiet and space to have your overdue chat!

2. Join in with a weekly hobby/activity one of your friends participates in. For example, if they go to an exercise class, volunteer at a local community group, or go running in the park – challenge yourself to join them in something that is part of their routine. And if you are considering taking up a new hobby post wedding (highly recommended), this is a good time to investigate the possibilities

3. Sit down with a cuppa (or a glass of wine or a cocktail if that's a fun way for you to unwind), and insist on some undivided together time with friends who you want to hear the latest from. Who had a funny date? What was the

> best night out? How did the charity fun run go
> and when is the next one? This should be a no
> technology (phone, tablet etc) zone so that you
> can enjoy each other's undivided attention.
> 4.   Dedicate 30–45 minutes a week to making calls
> to members of your family that you are keen
> to keep in touch with post-wedding. Wherever
> they are in the world, this means that your
> reconnection will last beyond your wedding day

Networking: professional

*Network continually – 85 percent of all jobs are filled
through contacts and personal references."*

Brian Tracy

To hit the post-wedding productivity zone, it is not just personal networks that need reviewing. On the career front, reconnecting with professional networks is the fastest route to reclaiming our sense of self.

*"Position yourself as a centre of influence, the one who
knows the movers and shakers. People will respond to that,
and you'll soon become what you project."*

Bob Burg

The quotes above make a very important point. Networking is essential for business success. If you still see career success as something which remains important to you after marriage, then professional networking is a must.

London based networking guru Bella Rareworld agrees. She helps business owners, SMEs and employers to maximise their networking for lead generation. She also works closely with women, teaching them how to use networking when job hunting and to achieve career goals and explains:

> *Networking is an essential activity for developing a network contact base or our 'black book'. On a regular basis we need to network to meet new people. Networking should be maximised because new contacts we meet can provide advice, support and introductions to help achieve goals in our personal or professional lives.*

She also notes that:

> *the wider and more diverse your network the better because there is potential to learn something new from each person. Networking can be an advantage because there are opportunities to get around gatekeepers. Networking is also a useful environment for keeping abreast with trends, sharing experiences, learning something new and testing ideas.*

This is not a revolutionary idea. It is not the first time, nor will it be the last, that someone tells you that for enhanced and accelerated career success, networking is essential.

Am I right? I know that if I were to take a guess as to excuses for not networking, the reasons would look something like this:

- Networking is superficial and networkers can be very self-absorbed

- Standing in a room with people I don't know has never gained me business
- I never know what to say to people in a networking situation
- I have better things to do with my time
- I'm too shy and nervous to go to networking events
- The people in the room are not my target audience
- The only benefit to networking is the free food and drink
- I don't like pushing myself on others.

If you are surprised by how accurately I have diagnosed your objections to networking, don't worry. I have not taken residence in your head, but these are some of the same reservations I used to have and I know we are by no means unique with these concerns and frustrations.

If you want to make a positive, rapid move towards post-wedding career progression, it is time for you to change your mindset and the great news is that it won't take too much to do so. All you need to do is redefine what you think professional networking is supposed to be. It is important to realise that networking:

- Happens everywhere – it is not just specific events
- Is not a quick fix!
- Is not a race in which the aim is to exchange as many business cards as possible in a short space of time
- Will not always provide all of your ideal clients/target audience in one room
- Is not all about you

- Is not about pushing yourself on someone or others pushing themselves on to you
- Is not always right for you (in other words, networking is right for you but not every group is the right fit for your aims, so you have to kiss a few frogs before you meet your networking prince).

What networking is all about is building relationships. And it is through the formation of solid relationships that some of your career aspirations can start to come to fruition. It can also have a positive impact on others as it is essential to 'give' as part of the process.

> *"The currency of real networking is*
> *not greed but generosity."*
>
> Keith Ferrazzi

Bella, our networking expert reiterates this, explaining that:

- It is important to understand re-connecting your network is not an overnight success. Networking success is a long-term achievement.
- Networking does not just take place at networking events, networking can occur anywhere and everywhere, such as the doctor's surgery, in a crowded ladies room, waiting for a bus/tube etc.
- Networking should not just stop when you achieve career goals. It's extraordinary, but the more successful you become in your career the more you need to network. When you move up the career ladder connecting within the right circles is powerful because it is all about "who you know" that

can open doors for you.

- It is important not to stop networking when the event is finished. Get motivated to continue to develop links with your existing network to keep the relationship fresh.

With that in mind, here are some top networking tips and a professional networking challenge.

Bella's top three networking tips for career-minded newlyweds:

1. Take some time to research the delegates booked to attend networking events. Request a copy of the attendee list before the event. Find out who will be attending, what are their job titles and industry sector. During the networking event you will be viewed as being professional because you have some background information about the delegates.

2. Be prepared by writing down some networking questions and answers. At a networking event you never know where the conversation will lead or what you might be asked. Before the networking event, practice your questions and answers out loud, this will help your networking conversation to have a nice flow.

3. Create a minimum of three networking goals. What do you want to achieve when networking? Is there a particular industry sector you are going to target? Who do you want to meet at the networking event? When you create networking goals it will give you focus and a sense of direction.

Karen Williams, business coach and mentor, author, speaker, and firewalk instructor, also recognises the importance of networks on all levels:

These days, networking is key to job change and career development. It's not what you know it's who you know. It's not enough to just apply for jobs in the paper or online as you will face competition from hundreds of other people. Also the best jobs involve you being in the right place at the right time, having the right conversations with those people in your networks or those of the people who you know.

In reference to re-establishing networks after couples have celebrated their big day, she says:

Personally I think it is important to keep your networks going all the time, rather than just resurrecting them when you need them. The purpose of having a network is helping others as well as asking for help yourself. However, if you do have a new name, it's worth reminding people who you are and your married name.

Karen's top three networking tips for career-minded newlyweds are:

1. Keep your LinkedIn profile up to date and include your skills, knowledge and what you are looking for.
2. If you are looking for a new job, tell your friends and those connections who are not directly related to work. (Of course, you can tell your work connections too if you feel comfortable

doing so). Have a clear understanding of what type of work and organisation you are looking to work for.

3.   Be clear on your elevator pitch which will enable you to be clear on your skills and talents and what you want. You never know when you may wish to share this – at the school gate, in a playground, at the gym, or in a party.

Networking exercise 2:

Create at least three face to face professional networking opportunities for yourself that you will participate in during the next three months. Remember, networking does not necessarily mean attending a bespoke networking event (though it would be good if attending one of these evenings is on your list). This can include meeting an old colleague for a coffee, approaching a potential mentor (a professional you admire), or offering to speak at a networking group or a lunchtime session at the office.

Make sure that you:

- Set an intention for the networking each time so you can make sure you leave feeling like you have accomplished something
- Find something you wouldn't mind going back to in the future.

Networking: social

Those who insert themselves into as many channels as possible look set to capture the most value. They'll be the richest, the most successful, the most connected, capable and influential among us. We're all publishers now, and the more we publish, the more valuable connections we'll make."

Pete Cashmore

We have established that personal and professional networking is important for newlyweds in making the shift from the post-wedding blues to post-wedding productivity. This is because taking specific steps towards widening our spheres of influence means that we are in the best possible position to positively refer others and be referred within our career areas.

However, when we think of networking these days we tend to exclusively think of social networking, neglecting the importance of face to face networking, which is why I deliberately leave the social aspect of networking until the end.

"How can you squander even one more day not taking advantage of the greatest shifts of our generation? How dare you settle for less when the world has made it so easy for you to be remarkable?"

Seth Godin

Social Networking can be personally or professionally focused and for career-driven newlyweds, it is something that should be embraced.

Karen Williams agrees and she reiterates, *"Social media is becoming increasingly important too, especially the professional network, LinkedIn. If you want to be connected with the CEO of a particular organisation, who do you know who can connect you?"*

Yes, there is a minority of people who may still insist social networking is a fad, but that was also said about the Internet years ago and look how wrong those sceptics were! By actively opting out of the constructive use of social media, you are deliberately putting yourself in a position where you miss out on career advancing opportunities and developments. How do you benefit from excluding yourself from receiving opportunities via these newer channels? Hint: you don't.

Take the time to get to know a bit about LinkedIn, Facebook, Twitter, Google+, YouTube, Ecademy and more and establish which ones will be your priority when it comes to developing your professional profile. Don't try it all at once but do set specific goals in terms of what you hope to achieve professionally on social networking and start working towards doing so.

It's hard to dwell in a potential post-wedding slump when you have such specific and important goals to be working towards. The networking-focused post-wedding blues-busting strategy being applied in this chapter feeds into the wider ways of achieving a level of productivity soon after you have said "I do".

Networking exercise 3:
How to kick your own butt – be your own coach

Until you get your own coach (or between coaching sessions), ask yourself these questions if you feel your enthusiasm diminishing when it comes to focusing on networking related aspirations:

- How might I benefit from strengthening my networks?

  _____

  _____

  _____

- Adversely, how will I benefit from **not** making the effort to strengthen my networks?

  _____

  _____

  _____

- What three things can I do to make the process of attending networking events more productive and less painful for me?

  _____

  _____

  _____

  _____

- What steps do I need to take to become the sort of person who becomes a 'go-to' person for others?

  _____

  _____

  _____

- List five positives you will gain from your next networking encounter.

1. _____

   _____

2. _____

   _____

3. _____

   _____

4. _____

   _____

5. _____

   _____

Chapter **5**

Partnership: Strengthen your union

"Almost no one is foolish enough to imagine that he automatically deserves great success in any field of activity; yet almost everyone believes that he automatically deserves success in marriage."

Sydney J. Harris

"We were perfectly happy until we decided to live happily ever after."

Carrie Bradshaw, Sex and the City (movie), 2008

At varying points in our lives we discover that things we were told in our childhood were made up. That's right – they were not true, they were false. These fibs (alright, whopping great lies) were delivered with the best of intentions – usually to make us feel happier. And quite often this 'story' had been perpetuated over generations so who were we to stop telling the tale?

You know the stories I mean. The idea that on Christmas Eve, a jolly man called Santa Claus shimmies down chimneys, leaves presents desired by the children of the house and sometimes indulges in some milk and cookies. Another is the idea that when you lose a tooth, the tooth fairy collects it and leaves some money in its place. Yet another is the idea that the Easter Bunny... well, I never knew what the Easter Bunny did apart from share chocolate and wear flamboyant hats. But you understand the point I am trying to make...

Through our childhoods we often happily indulged in these tales of joy designed to entertain and please. Yet the one that we didn't entirely shake as a children's fairytale is the concept of 'happily ever after' when it comes to a man and a woman. This one has stuck with us and is one of the reasons why, in taking action to beat the post-wedding blues, it is essential to take a closer look at what our wedding and marriage expectations are.

"So it's not gonna be easy. It's gonna be really hard. We're gonna have to work at this every day, but I want to do that because I want you. I want all of you, forever, you and me, every day..."

Young Noah, The Notebook (movie)

Remember... the post-wedding blues describe that temporary yet inexplicably empty feeling we can sometimes experience after our wedding day. It is no reflection on your partner or your marriage – it is an anti-climactic, temporary slump that can be disheartening after celebrating such a momentous occasion.

In this chapter, we will look at a number of elements which will serve to strengthen our partnership and in turn, help overcome any lingering post-wedding blues.

This chapter will explore:
- What marriage is – traditional and modern definitions
- Keeping fun alive
- Time management, goals and togetherness.

Through looking at the above, we will establish the secret of blues-busting togetherness, strengthening your partnership.

What is marriage – traditional and modern definitions?

"One advantage of marriage is that, when you fall out
of love with him or he falls out of love with you,
it keeps you together until you fall in again."
Judith Viorst

"Happy is the man who finds a true friend, and far happier
is he who finds that true friend in his wife."
Franz Schubert

One of the most important steps in banishing the post-wedding blues is reminding yourself what marriage is and what it means to you as a couple. You have just taken this life transforming step – and have not done so lightly. So, beyond throwing an awesome party for your family and friends, what was the big picture behind you wanting to be married? What does marriage mean for you?

According to the Oxford English Dictionary, marriage is *"the formal union of a man and a woman, typically as recognized by law, by which they become husband and wife."*

Marriage for me is that – yes – but so so much more. To me, marriage is a sacred institution which constitutes a promise of love, honour and faithfulness between two people. It is a partnership created between two people who want to share a life through all of its ups and downs – knowing that whatever life throws their way, they want to face it together. For me, marriage does not automatically fall into place after a glorious wedding day. Rather, the stated marriage vows highlight the intent and the union. Then, they become a series of constant choices and clear communication between a couple who know that they may be fantastic people on their own but they are even better when they are together.

Doing research for this book, I was honoured to gain an insight into the meaning of marriage according to others I spoke to and here is what they believe:

Shazmin, Kenya:

> *Marriage is a new life....it's a new beginning....it's when you are truly grown-up and have to take responsibility for yourself and your partner. Life is no longer about me but now about US! It's a commitment for life...it's about compromise and sacrifice....learning to grow as an individual and as a couple – a new family unit. Marriage is about ups and downs, happy moments and sad moments, good days and bad days. Understanding how to deal with this, everything life*

has in store for you AND your partner is what marriage is about.

Carolina, Germany/UK:

Marriage is a commitment to someone and to a part of yourself. The part which includes balance, hard-work, the reforming of habits, bit by bit. It's the backbone of family. It is something I had always wanted because I want a family.

Ida, Finland / USA

We struggled to define and put parameters around that huge word: Marriage. It comes with so many connotations - religious, cultural, legal, gendered - it's no wonder books are written about it. We found that the more we tried to "make sense" of marriage, the more we got bogged down in The Expectations that capital "M" marriage entails. The stereotypes go like this: when you get Married, you are Expected to settle down; combine your finances, start saving, and investing; buy a house; behave in a "husband and wife" manner (whatever that means!); have children; change your wills; co-sign birthday cards; share holiday visits between families; and hang out with other married couples. Some of those Expectations didn't mesh with our lifestyle or self-images as partners at all; others were already effortlessly happening. But significantly, we did not deem it necessary to be Married to do any (or none) of the above... but chose to get married due to the practicalities of being from different countries and wanting to be together.

Fariba, UK/Canada:

Marriage is the ultimate commitment, a milestone in a relationship, partnership which is forever. I'm a romantic and an idealist and I just loved the idea of having someone to grow old with, to share everything with, to have a family with, to be your best friend and partner for the rest of your life. I love that I am growing with my husband and I always look forward to the future with him.

Helen, Canada:

To me, marriage means a profound level of commitment and understanding, having someone who loves you no matter what, and who will be there for you through thick and thin. He's definitely my biggest supporter, and I am his.

Katy, UK:

My marriage to my husband means everything and more. I married my life partner, soul mate, best friend and the most amazing father.

Jeannine, Jamaica/Canada:

For me marriage was always about partnership. Two individuals becoming stronger once they loved each other and worked together. It is something that I saw in my parents growing up and definitely always wanted for myself.

Julie, UK:

Marriage to me means sharing my life with someone

which means unconditional love. It should also mean I can grow as a person with another person who supports and understand and encourages me. For me it is the same. I want my own identity but share my life with a like-minded soul.

Rebecca, UK

Marriage means having another person to share your life with e.g. your thoughts, feelings, experiences and goals (both bad and good). It is about providing a sense of containment and committing yourself, for life, to someone else. It is about putting someone else's needs before your own. For me it means to feel supported, valued and respected and that you are not alone. Companionship, friendship, passion, shared values and experiences are words that come to mind.

Anita, Guyana/Canada:

For me, marriage it's about love, commitment, trust, security and support. It is knowing that someone will always be there for you, no matter what the circumstances are. It's having someone to come home to at the end of a crazy day and laughing with for no good reason.

Elizabeth, USA/UK:

Marriage means so many different things to me, and it has a way of changing every day. In the purist sense, I define it as an equal and loving partnership, a lifetime commitment filled with more happiness than sadness. When I think of marriage I think of complete support given to, and received from, my partner. I think of lots of laughing and also knowing that when things got tough (as they inevitably do) that we would find a way to get to a better place again together. Plus, lots of sex! Admittedly, there are other days I think about marriage as having someone to make a cup of tea when I'm tired, or intuitively knowing when I'm cold and turning on the heating without a single exchange between us. It's about that seamless dance between two people who simply understand each other.

I do tend to think of 'marriage' as interchangeable with 'loving partnership', which I also felt I had pre-ceremony. I didn't think that getting married would change the way I felt about my partner. It did, and it didn't. The 'crazy in love' and 'I'm so lucky' feelings are still there and I never once doubted we would always be together. But now that we're married with an official piece of paper, there is a deeper sense of permanence I didn't think was possible to have but now do.

Sharmeen, USA:

It means security but not in a trapped kind of way. It means love and support with another partner. Someone who accepts who I am fully and works with me towards improving each other and us, and also pushing me to pursue my goals.

Alex, UK

Marriage is a way of committing to another person, and committing to share everything in life with them. I had always wanted to get married although do not believe it defines your relationship. I think it helps bring stability but not a greater connection.

Priyanka, India:

Marriage means having this one person in your life at all times – good and bad, someone to share your life with even if it meant making small sacrifices in your career and independence. Marriage is about working on a relationship and growing together as different individuals with a common outlook towards life. I did want to get married, a little because of my culture (you need to get married to settle down) but also because I wanted a companion to love and cherish for life. Someone I could talk to about anything at any time of the day or night. Someone to cuddle whose arms would make the world a better place.

Marsha, Trinidad / UK:

Marriage is that declaration to the world that you have found your perfect partner to salsa with, and even though you'll probably tread on each other's toes, or spin away or not want to dance sometimes, you each are wholeheartedly committed to getting back in step. There is no judging, so you're free to be yourself, because you are beautiful to that person and the best you can be ALWAYS!

Los Angeles-based newlyweds Micaela and Ed Cunje also reflected on what marriage means to them and certainly seem to be on the same page regarding their expectations.

Michaela:

I did always want to be married. Before my father passed away in 2007, my parents were married for 35 years, and always experienced how wonderful a marriage and family could be. For me, marriage is a life-long commitment to the person you love to always love, care for, be loyal to, have fun with and cherish them. It doesn't mean always being happy, but it means being happier with them than without them.

Ed:

Marriage has always been important to me. I have grown-up watching my parents, married for well over 30 years, as a shining example of true love. I learned a lot about life from them and I hope that one day I will have an opportunity to share what I have learned. Marriage is a bond, a compromise between two people, agreeing to spend the rest of their lives together.

Co-founders of Ecademy, (the UK's first business social network) and married for more than twenty years, entrepreneurial couple, the Powers, also contributed to the discussion. Penny Power says *"marriage to me is a lifelong journey of unconditional love and belief in your partner".* Her husband, Thomas Power, says *"for me marriage is the foundation of my life."*

I feel truly honoured to have shared conversations at this level with a range of people, from newlyweds to some of the UK's most renowned business people and personalities. I know that these varying definitions of what marriage is are potentially beneficial in any newlywed's bid to surpass their temporary post-wedding motivational slump.

The above provides plenty of inspiration about the significance of marriage, and in a bid to banish the post-wedding blues, it is important that you establish and communicate your own definitions.

With that in mind, take the time to complete this exercise:

Blues-busting togetherness exercise 1
Definitions and significance of marriage

1. What does marriage mean to me?

    • _____
       _____
    • _____
       _____
    • _____
       _____
       _____
    • _____
       _____

2. What are the reasons that I choose marriage
    every day?

    • _____
       _____
    • _____
       _____
    • _____
       _____
    • _____
       _____

Keeping fun alive

*"It is not a lack of love, but a lack of friendship
that makes unhappy marriages."*

Friedrich Nietzsche

While signing official marriage papers suggests that togetherness is a done deal once you have said "I do" – ever frightening divorce statistics suggest quite the opposite. UK divorce statistics released by the Office of National Statistics in December 2012 confirm that the number of divorces in England and Wales in 2011 was 117,558. A November 2012 report by The Marriage Foundation highlights that celebrities are twice as likely to divorce as the rest of the married UK population, with 40% of celebrities getting divorced within 10 years as opposed to 20% of the general population.

> The report, written by relationships expert Harry Benson and family law Barrister Rehna Azim, argues that the celebrity culture absorbed from magazines like *Hello!* give us unrealistic, fairy-tale expectations about marriage and relationships, when in fact, "… the glamour of celebrity weddings is a poor indicator of future marital success." The Marriage Foundation examined 572 well-known celebrity couples who have tied the knot since the year 2000. The report highlights the weddings of celebrities such as Britney Spears, whose marriage to Jason Alexander lasted just 55 hours. It concludes that people should have more accurate expectations of how much hard work it takes to keep a marriage together.

So what does it take? There is no one size fits all answer for every couple and certainly no guarantee of happily ever after but taking the time to have fun together is bound to have a positive impact on a marriage. In this section, we explore the many reasons why couples should ensure they sustain the fun of their relationship in their marriage. After all, it's harder to feel blue when you're having a great time.

"Marriage is the beginning, not the end of the party!"

Gina Visram

Like me, you may have also noticed that there is a very strange culture surrounding the notion of marriage. It is often communicated and perceived as the beginning of the end – instead of the beginning of a new adventure.

Have you noticed the same? The hen and stag night (bachelor and bachelorette) party culture is often referred to as the last night of freedom, which I understand (in theory) in terms of freedom of partners, but entirely disagree with in terms of freedom of lifestyle. Surely, you want the person you married to be the same (or at least resemble) the person you were initially attracted to and later fell in love with. Therefore, if you would have described them as "fun loving" and "the life of the party" at any stage, you are likely to be disappointed if some of what you fell in love with ceases to exist after your wedding day.

With that in mind, there are a few lighter hearted "I dos" that couples should incorporate into their marriage. Look at each other and repeat after me:

- At the beginning of our marriage, I do promise to

take the time to reflect on some of the favourite things that we enjoyed before our wedding [list them] and work to make sure they don't disappear from our lives!

- I do promise to share at least a laugh a day with you
- I do promise to make the time to enjoy regular date nights
- I do promise to find a shared activity/hobby that we can enjoy together
- I do promise to see new places and enjoy new adventures with you
- I do promise to respect and encourage your desire to spend time with your friends (separate from me)
- I do promise to make the effort to spend time with your friends and family at appropriate occasions
- I do promise to encourage fun nights out on the town… whether together as a couple or independently with our varying friendship groups.

What do you think? While these are not vows that we make during our wedding ceremony, they are promises we can make which will ensure that the fun is maintained in marriage.

Your stag/hen night should not be the last night you hit the club, enjoy a tequila shot (if that's your thing) or dance until dawn. For as long as you consider this to be an enjoyable way to spend your time, you should allow yourself the luxury of enjoying moments like this as they will make you happy. Two happy individuals who also work on their shared interests and shared goals will go a long way to making a happy couple.

Beyond this, people embarking on marriage would do well to consider what freedom means to them. If freedom constitutes being intimate with anyone other than your spouse or doing literally anything you want to do whenever you want to do it (with no compromise) then it is likely that marriage is not for you at this time. If however, your concept of freedom incorporates the scope to enjoy life to the full with your greatest supporter by your side, then you are on to a good thing. You can smile, shake your head and mock the sceptics who view marriage in this way:

> *"What do you call the three rings of marriage?*
> *The engagement ring, the wedding ring,*
> *and the suffering."*

Cedric, Think Like a Man (movie), 2012

Get ready for much fun ahead and you can start by doing the exercise below:

Blues-busting togetherness exercise 2
Activities and adventure

What were my favourite activities before I got married? What activities which are personal to me bring a smile to my face/make me relax? (These can include *Zumba*/ dance class, playing team sports etc.)

_____

_____

_____

> What adventures would I like us to share in the next
> 1–3 years?
>
> _____
>
> _____
>
> _____
>
> _____

Time Management and Togetherness

"What's the use of a marriage when nothing is shared?"

Evelyn Greenslade,
The Best Exotic Marigold Hotel, (movie), 2011

*"Tomorrow is the only day in the year that
appeals to a lazy man."*

Jimmy Lyon

While marriage doesn't constitute being joined at the hip at all times, exploring the areas of time management, goals and togetherness are an important element of busting the post-wedding blues and achieving a feeling of being settled in the early days of your marriage.

Let's start with time management. Our ability in this area actually affects all aspects of our lives (including how we manage our careers). Naturally, it also affects our bond within our marriage which is why it is worth exploring here.

*"Today is the word for winners and tomorrow
is the word for losers."*

Robert Kiyosaki

We live in an era where the nuclear family concept is a fluid one. No more is it necessarily a man and a woman, two point something kids, a car and a white picket fence. Instead, we live in an era where any or all of these scenarios are likely to be true:

- The couple/family lives away from other relatives
- The two people in the marriage both work (be it in employment or for themselves etc)
- Husband and wife live in different cities or countries
- A couple may live with wider family
- A couple may have a baby/kids/stepchildren before their wedding
- Wife/husband or both may have more than one job or work at differing times of the day.

As a result of these and many more scenarios for married couples these days, it is not possible to take togetherness for granted. That is why, in researching this book a key question I asked was "How good are you at balancing time for yourself and time for being together?"

The answers are below and they highlight that time management and togetherness vary greatly between couples:

Shazmin, Kenya:

*'Me' time has never been a priority in my life....
it's always about everyone else. As long as I can give*

enough time to 'us' then I have taken care of the 'me' time.

Sharmeen, USA:

Still working it out, but I think I do well. We both like spending our "hangout out" time with one another. But if we both need some space, the other respects it or at least understands it. It will get easier over time but also right now I love spending my time with him as well.

Carolina, Germany/UK:

Struggle a lot with this one.

Helen, Canada:

Pretty good – we have very different work schedules sometimes, so we really value our time together (usually on weekends) and try to make the most of it.

Bethan, UK:

We used to work different hours until recently so we are both used to time apart. I sometimes travel with work, so that's also normal. We make time to be together but also respect each other's space and have one or two evenings apart every week. This isn't planned time apart for the sake of being away from each other, just time for hobbies. For example, I have no interest in cricket…

Elizabeth, UK/USA:

Since falling pregnant, I've spent more evenings at home than I did previously so we've had a lot more together time. I find that at the moment I want to spend as much free time with my partner as possible, though I still enjoy taking time for myself whether that's being out and about with friends or hitting the gym.

Salma, UK:

I've never stopped in my tracks and thought 'Oh I don't spent enough time on my own,' as I'm not one of those people who needs that; I prefer to socialise. Every month my husband and I have at least one date out and weekly we make a point of cooking a really nice meal together. We have time with our friends and he also gets to play his computer games when I'm working on planning lessons at the weekend. I think we've got it worked out quite nicely to be honest!

Priyanka, India:

Very good. I prioritise family and work and am able to manage quite well.

Jessica, USA:

Not as good as I should be. Because of work schedules and the few days of the week he plays sports after work, I typically want to spend any time we do have free together. I can't help it, I have so much fun with him and I love spending time with him. I probably should set aside more time for myself and will – but it has been challenging since most weekends are spent with friends/family or doing errands together. I definitely need a 'me' day in the near future.

Nicola, UK:

Pretty good. My husband is studying for some big IT exams, so we are both quite busy, but we have a routine, and we talk a lot, so the time together does feel like quality time.

Lexi, UK:

Sometimes very good and sometimes terrible. Mostly somewhere in between.

Jeannine, Jamaica/Canada:

That is one of the hardest parts of being a wife and mother. There are not enough hours in a day and time for me always comes last. I have to make a special effort to make time for the two of us as well.

Pamela:

Sometimes we are better at this than others. Lately, we have been a horrible example of this because we have been so busy with the house. But, we try to eat dinner together almost every night, we always go to bed together, and we are working on doing a "date night" (in or out) at least once per month.

What do these shared experiences tell us? The variety of responses highlight that there is no normal or fixed way to be in a marriage. What becomes clear is the fact that we should not be putting ourselves under any undue pressure when we are married to create the ideal of how a married couple spends time together. There is no one way to be. Instead, what is essential is that you address how you want to be as a couple. What are *your* expectations – not those of your parents, generations before, your friends your siblings or anyone else – what commitments do you want to make to each other to ensure you are happy with the quality of the time you spend together?

"Don't be fooled by the calendar. There are only as many days in the year as you make use of. One man gets only a week's value out of a year while another man gets a full year's value out of a week."

Charles Richards

"Ordinary people think merely of spending time. Great people think of using it."

Author Unknown

"Take care of the minutes and the hours will take care of themselves."

Lord Chesterfield

As each couple is so different the only real formula to getting this right is to make sure that you communicate with each other about what you want and expect. I can't speak for others but as you may find it beneficial to have an illustration of what I mean, see below for some definite markers of success that R and I use when it comes to quality togetherness time. Some of these include:

- Having a date night at least once a month (we are aiming to raise that to twice a month)
- Having positive discussions about our upcoming day in the ten-minute car journey we do together on weekday mornings
- Cooking together
- Eating together at least three times a week
- Travelling to a destination we haven't been to before once a year (if finances don't allow this to be overseas, somewhere within the UK works for us)
- Meet (at our dining table or on our sofa) once a month to discuss our career ups and downs
- Cuddling on the sofa and watching a DVD once a month
- Enjoying a hobby together (we are still working towards achieving this more regularly)
- Participate in a business focused seminar/workshop together twice a year.

"We need a witness to our lives. There's a billion people on the planet, what does any one life really mean? But in a marriage, you're promising to care about everything. The good things, the bad things, the terrible things, the mundane things, all of it, all of the time, every day. You're saying 'Your life will not go unnoticed because I will notice it. Your life will not go unwitnessed because I will be your witness'."

Beverly Clark, Shall we Dance (movie), 2004

**Blues-busting togetherness exercise 3:
Time management and togetherness**

What does quality time together mean for me? (Is it eating together with the TV off, having a regular date night etc?)

_____

_____

_____

_____

_____

_____

If time were no object, what three things would we love to do together on a regular basis?

_____

_____

_____

_____

_____

_____

Even if you are not currently managing to achieve the level of togetherness you want, as long as you are both clear that you are headed in the same direction and are seeking to achieve the same thing, this is a very positive start. The importance of focused, as opposed to accidental, togetherness is a key aspect of overcoming any feelings of post-wedding blues/post-wedding lack of motivation.

Goals

> *"We both said, 'I do!' and we haven't agreed on a single thing since."*
>
> Stuart Mackenzie, *So I Married an Axe Murderer* (movie), 1993

> *"The key is in not spending time, but in investing it."*
>
> Stephen R. Covey

> *"The goal in marriage is not to think alike, but to think together."*
>
> Robert C. Dodds

> *"My wife has been my closest friend, my closest advisor. And ... she's not somebody who looks to the limelight, or even is wild about me being in politics. And that's a good reality check on me. When I go home she wants me to be a good father and a good husband. And everything else is secondary to that."*
>
> Barack Obama

I imagine that some of the 'quality time and togetherness' markers I shared with you may resonate in terms of some of what you and your partner strive to achieve... and you will be completely disinterested in others. That is exactly how it should be. Each couple's measure of quality together time will be different because it is important that some of these factors tie into the goals of the individuals in the relationship and the joint aspirations of the couple.

In the case of me and my husband, things like going to business seminars together constitute quality time together because R runs his own business and I am working towards a similar goal. As a result, some memorable and enjoyable occasions we have spent together have been at seminars which have been thought provoking, taught us something and generated great conversation, debate and actions which will take us closer to our goals.

Little actions such as communicating our main aims for the day in the morning and writing down successes at the end of the day – which we then read to each other – are actions which bring us close together as a couple. Since we feel like we are striving together towards our goals, these actions make us happy.

Chapter 3 provides clear information about how to set SMART goals... so use this formula in setting goals individually and together.

This chapter, 'Blues-Busting Togetherness: Strengthen Your Partnership' has been designed to highlight that making plans/organising dates with each other should not stop because you live together or because you are married. Being married does not automatically equal quality time. In a bid to achieve motivation beyond an initial post-wedding slump in productivity, it is important to put in the work.

Blues-busting togetherness exercise 4
Keep a success diary

Buy two notebooks (one for you and your spouse) and use them to capture your successes at the end of each day.

Just before you go to sleep, write at least three things that you are proud to have achieved during the day. They can be as small as choosing a salad instead of chips for lunch, doing an exercise DVD in the morning before work, or achieving the main goals you set at work that day.

Anything you are proud of should qualify to be written in the book.

Once you have both written yours down, read them to each other. It's a lovely way to end each day!

Chapter **6**

Investigate your career: Do a Career Audit

"I've yet to be on a campus where most women weren't worrying about some aspect of combining marriage, children, and a career. I've yet to find one where many men were worrying about the same thing."

Gloria Steinem

It is not uncommon to hear the question 'can women have it all?' This discussion has been ever present as far back as I can remember and it shows no sign of ceasing – even at this point in the 21st century.

The quote above struck a chord with me as it highlights the reasons why the topics in this book may resound with modern working wives. These days, women often:

- Get married later in life – and therefore spend many years building their career credibility before settling down with their prince
- Would like to keep building their careers after they have started having a family
- Need to think creatively about how to balance the varying aspects of their lives – all of which are important

- Feel that there needs to be a decision made between baby and career – not necessarily knowing how to successfully combine the two.

In assessing our current careers, these are all aspects to be considered. So, what are the things we need to do in our career path to ensure we are on track with a career we can be proud of?

In this chapter, we will look at how to:

- Do a career audit – and understand why it is important
- Create a link between career auditing and our own version of happily ever after.

By the end of this chapter, you will have a better sense of:

- Your values and beliefs: are your career and married life a match made in heaven? Have your values and priorities changed?
- How to approach your boss about a promotion/ pay rise
- Top tips for job hunting in any market (including using Twitter and LinkedIn)
- Unusual interview tips
- The kind of support available in your bid to make positive steps in developing your career (a mentor, coach etc)
- Dealing with any changing aspirations you may have, embracing the different career development tools at your disposal – including social media – if you do have a promotion or new job that you are striving for.

The link between career auditing and happily ever after...

*"Not only is women's work never done,
the definition keeps changing."*

Bill Copeland

*"A career is wonderful, but you can't
curl up with it on a cold night."*

Marilyn Monroe

The idea of writing this book actually came to me at an event called the 'National Achievers Congress' (NAC), an event held in one of the largest exhibition venues in London. The line-up was phenomenal with headliners including Anthony Robbins, life coach and world authority on leadership psychology; Lord Sugar, British business magnate; and another British business magnate Richard Branson all talked about their journey and shared their wealth of knowledge with the audience to inspire them to achieve their own goals.

At the point of attending this event, I had been married for just over two months and was looking for ways to motivate myself to get my career coaching initiative back on track. I was feeling a touch out of sorts and had become somewhat disconcerted that in the few months since the wedding, I was not achieving what I thought I should be at that stage in career terms.

This was unlike me. After all, in the wedding planning phase, I multitasked effectively enough to work in a demanding full-time PR agency job, complete my personal performance coaching qualification and even write content for and launch the website for my coaching initiative, Limitless Coaching. I had also found, and was settling into, a new communications and marketing job, which I started five weeks before our wedding – all while working hard on the planning of our big day.

My track record meant I had absolutely no doubt in my capacity to successfully balance a number of things at once. However, I found that in this very early stage of my marriage, I was managing to have productive days at work and doing some exercise. Yet in terms of my other aspirations, I felt a malaise I was unfamiliar with – and refused to give in to it any longer than I had already.

This was actually my reason for signing up for the NAC as I anticipated that between the amazing speakers, the energy in the room and actually doing something completely out of the ordinary, I would regain my mojo and get back to being my best.

You may or may not have noticed from my description of this slump in my motivation levels that it had nothing to do with the amazing man I married. But it did follow the incredible celebrations (in the UK and Guyana) of our union – a seeming result of the anti-climax of our return to the daily grind.

With a clear understanding that I was not feeling remotely blue about my new marriage (quite the opposite actually!), it became clear to me that to return to my best self, I needed to take some time to be introspective. This involved doing a career audit and analysing my values and beliefs – on a personal and professional level. Here's what a career audit entails…

Audit your career: Where are you now and where would you like to be?

"It is all too easy to speed through life with our eyes focused only on the road ahead. The challenge is scanning the horizon from time to time to determine where we are headed."

Christopher Gergen and Gregg Vanourek

If you are a newlywed, chances are in the past months you have been focused on the motorway speeding towards your wedding day, but may not have slowed down to take in many other sights.

This intense focus on your personal life (the wedding planning) is a very different, much more 'personal life' focused approach than you may have ever had previously. This is because often, our focus has been the route taken from school, to university and beyond when the ultimate aim has been to build and grow our career opportunities. All of these make this time – the period just after you get married – the ideal time to scour the wider horizon and reassess those goals you have traditionally worked so hard towards.

In order to avoid speeding through life without a current assessment of what you want to be speeding towards, the career audit process is an important one as self-awareness helps ensure your career decisions are right for you. Start your career audit by completing the exercise here:

Career-Audit exercise 1:
Your post-wedding career audit

What is my job field and title?

_____

_____

How long have I been in the role and what does it
entail?

_____

_____

_____

How far does it meet the needs of what I am currently
seeking in terms of my career? In what ways does it suit
me?

_____

_____

_____

_____

_____

_____

When was the last time I focused on achieving my next
promotion and am I at a stage where I am currently
looking to progress in my career?

_____

_____

_____

_____

_____

_____

What are the career-related skills I am most proud of?

- _____
- _____
- _____
- _____
- _____

How far do I use these within my current role?

_____
_____
_____
_____

What motivates and fulfils me within my job?

- _____
- _____
- _____
- _____
- _____

How far do I agree with the following statement "I am proud to work for my employer"?

     Strongly agree

     Slightly agree

     Slightly disagree

     Strongly disagree

How far do I agree with the following statement "I would like more out of my career/job than I currently feel I am getting"?

    Strongly agree

    Slightly agree

    Slightly disagree

    Strongly disagree

How far do I agree with the following statement "I am constantly counting down the days and living for the weekend?"

    Strongly agree

    Slightly agree

    Slightly disagree

    Strongly disagree

How satisfied was I with my life (incorporating areas of career etc.) before my engagement? (See scale below where 1 is deeply unsatisfied and 10 is extremely satisfied) and why?

    1   2   3   4   5   6   7   8   9   10

_____

_____

_____

How satisfied was I with my life (incorporating areas of career etc) in the immediate months after my wedding? (1 is deeply unsatisfied and 10 is extremely satisfied) and why?

     1   2   3   4   5   6   7   8   9   10

_____

_____

_____

What three things can I do to bring myself an even better sense of career satisfaction?

1. _____
2. _____
3. _____

Work/life perspectives from real brides

Newlyweds interviewed for this book were kind enough to share their experience of their careers before and after marriage. They also reflect on whether they experienced a post-wedding slump in motivation and compare life before and after they said "I do".

Each story is so different and gives an insight into how some brides, from a variety of countries around the world, have worked to balance the most significant parts of their lives:

Nicola, UK

How active were you in your career/business/career development before the wedding?

I was a Marketing Officer in the Public Sector working full-time, with some freelance work in the evenings/ weekends.

I agree that when I was planning my wedding, I focused less on my career development than I otherwise would have.

How did you feel in the days and weeks following your wedding and honeymoon (i.e., when the wedding was officially over)?

I felt a bit lost initially; I suddenly had lots of free time on my hands. I thought I was going to have a honey-moon baby!?! When it didn't happen I felt really down. So I knew that I needed a project to occupy my mind. I had the idea for the blog – www.bellenoirbride.co.uk – about 3 months into my planning, so decided to throw myself into working on this blog which aims to inspire and reflect black brides more than mainstream media, as I now had the time and energy to devote to hopefully creating something I wish was around when I was embarking on my own wedding planning journey.

I think the post-wedding blues/post wedding slump is the void that is created when you suddenly have lots of time on your hands. It's the thinking 'what's next', marriage is a big stage and I know it certainly got me thinking about the next steps. Some of which cannot be controlled which then lends itself to the blues.

What has been your experience with the post-wedding slump in motivation?

Get a project! Throw yourself into doing something that makes you feel good. I suddenly found that I had this energy and desire to do more with my time and achieve more for the both of us. The blog has stopped me from really suffering from a post-wedding slump, and now with the plans I have to start a freelance career, I feel really good.

Since getting married, I have been most proud of making each other happy, starting the blog, and supporting each other. I am pretty good at balancing time for myself and time for being together. My husband is studying for some big IT exams, so we are both quite busy, but we have a routine, and we talk a lot, so the time together does feel like quality time.

Priyanka, India:

How active were you in your career/business/career development before the wedding?

I was working full-time with CNBC, India's first Hindi business channel. I was working full-time from 9–8. Journalists have no fixed working hours so sometimes longer.

Before my engagement I was an 8/10 on a satisfaction scale regarding my life. I was happy, work was good, I had friends for a fun social life. Life was busy but thought it was time to settle down.

How did you find the wedding planning process?

Culture in India is the parents plan the wedding from beginning to end so I had nothing much to do except shop for my clothes, accessories etc. and get pampered. The rest was all up to them because in India they are expected to and I guess want to do everything for your wedding. Here it's not just about the boy and girl but also about their families and their standing in society.

As a result, I slightly disagree that I focused less on my career development during the wedding planning time, as a result.

Since getting married I have changed jobs to give more time to family and balance work and personal life. Also, I have tried to be calmer and less impatient for small mundane things.

Life satisfaction after the wedding (incorporating career etc.) became a 7 because marriage is work, you have to work on it every day and especially the first few months in India can be a little hectic. You don't know what everybody expects from you and vice-versa. I was staying with my in-laws so I believe the adjustment period was a little more for me and them both.

For me, the post-wedding blues/post-wedding slump is about adjusting with a whole new family. They go out of their way to make you comfortable but sometimes the attention can be too much. I believe that because you don't know them and they don't know you it's very difficult to understand each other in the first few

*weeks/months/sometimes years. You're always on your
toes as the relationship is very formal. You need your
husband around to make you comfortable with them.*

*Since getting married, I am most proud of starting my
own media company with the help of my husband…
and I am very good at balancing time for myself and
time for being together. I prioritise family and work
and am able to manage quite well.*

Carolina, Germany/UK:

How active were you in your career/business/career
development before the wedding?

It was full-time, often very long hours.

*I agree that when I was planning my wedding, I
focused less on my career development than I otherwise
would have.*

*In my opinion, the post-wedding slump in motivation
was a matter of coming down off the emotion of the
wedding. I didn't have a long slump.*

Micaela, USA

How active were you in your career/business/career
development before the wedding?

*I was pretty active in my career, working full-time,
sometimes overtime. I am involved with most of the
training that is part of the company's thousand employees, from new hires to department-based enhancement
training.*

The wedding planning process was a lot of fun! Much more fun than what I had been told. There were definitely stressful moments, like the budget and guest list, but it was a lot more fun than it was stressful. We did a lot of the planning together and really enjoyed the process. I was a lot more calm than I thought I'd be, lol.

I strongly agree that when I was planning my wedding, I focused less on my career development than I otherwise would have.

How did you feel in the days and weeks following your wedding and honeymoon (i.e., when the wedding was officially over)?

I felt great! I was so happy and excited to start our life together. It was great to go to bed and wake up next to my husband! We relived our wedding for weeks, and then we got pictures and the video so we really got to revisit our beautiful day!

The first significant thing that we did on return from honeymoon was move in with Ed's parents so that we could start saving to buy our home. I had to move from my parents' and into Ed's parents' home. I was really excited that I was going to live with him. After that, I returned to work. It was pretty sad to go back to reality after spending that entire week with him and seeing him 24/7.

I don't know exactly what the post-wedding blues consist of, so I think I've been very lucky, but I imagine that it's a sadness that results from the change that comes with marriage. Your life changes from only

*revolving around you, where you don't have to think
of the other person as much, where you do things as
you've always done, to one where everything you do
affects your husband. It is a lot of responsibility and of
course, it can be difficult because you're learning to live
with your spouse, but I am lucky to have a very caring
husband who is super attentive and loving.*

*My personal experience was that I think I had lost
a bit of motivation because I was so happy spending
time with my husband, everything we did was exciting because we were doing it together. Now though, it
has actually motivated me to excel at work so that I
can make more money to buy our own home and start
preparing for kids.*

Lexi, UK

How active were you in your career/business/career
development before the wedding?

*I was very active in my career/business development
before the wedding. I was pursuing a new role on a
different team full-time (business development/creative
solutions rather than display ad sales). I was inter-
viewing and preparing for this in the run up to our
wedding day.*

*Before the wedding, I was a 7 on the satisfaction scale
– I enjoyed my role in display sales and was happy
in my personal life but was looking for progression in
both!*

How did you find the wedding planning process?

As we had a more traditional period of engagement (i.e., we took our time!) it was quite easy and relatively stress free. Everything just fell into place – our preferred venues were available and within our (very loose) budget. Family politics and a delay on my dress were the only pressure points but both were resolved with minimum fuss.

I strongly disagree that when I was planning my wedding, I focused less on my career development than I otherwise would have – I applied for and was then offered a new position at work during the period that we were engaged. My last day in my old position was the week before our wedding day and I started my new position fresh from our honeymoon.

In the days and weeks following the wedding I was on a high for some time, basking in the afterglow of the day and honeymoon. I also had a new job to look forward to. I know that some people find themselves disappointed that it's over or feel like they have a lot of spare time but nothing changed for me. I was ecstatic that I was now fully committed to the man I loved and that was more important than anything else.

After our wedding I moved up to a 9 on that satisfaction scale. I was excited about starting a new job! Like any time when you change positions, I was nervous but excited for the new challenge ahead. Since being married, nothing vital changed aside from continuing up the career ladder. We already owned a house, a pet...I

*still have a life outside of our marriage and so does he.
I simply get to refer to him as my husband rather than
my boyfriend or fiancé.*

*In my opinion, the post-wedding slump is when you
lose sight of what getting married is about. For me,
whilst I wanted things a certain way, this wasn't the
be all and end all. What was important was that I
was married to the man I loved and that our friends
and family were there to share that with us. If the 'day'
hadn't have been exactly perfect, it really wouldn't have
destroyed the sentiment behind why we were doing it.
Fixating on the smallest details will overtake your life
and so of course, when you have nothing left to fixate
on you will naturally feel a loss. Some people also seem
to have fantastical ideas about how getting married
will change their relationship beyond recognition. They
lack a sense of realism and so believe that everything
will be perfect even if it wasn't before.*

*Since getting married, I am most proud of the way
we have built our lives together. I would like to think
that people look at us as a strong and stable couple who
really understand what works for us.*

Jeannine, Jamaica/Canada

How active were you in your career/business/career
development before the wedding?

*When we first started planning the wedding I was in
Medical school full-time and he was in Architecture
school full-time. Closer to the actual wedding day he was*

working full-time and I was at home with the baby.

I was about an 8 on the career/life satisfaction scale before marriage. I was excited about my career and about my life with him however I had no idea how it was all going to come together considering we were from different parts of the world (remember I tend to be a little bit of a control freak). I still did not feel settled and longed for the feeling of belonging and stability I missed growing up moving around all over the world.

I found the wedding planning process to be fun at first, on paper. The actual budget, finalizing and the guest list were a nightmare. It was just tedious work. By the wedding day we were both so happy, partially because the planning part was over. Our wedding was a beautiful day and I will always remember it fondly.

I slightly agree that when I was planning my wedding, I focused less on my career development than I otherwise would have.

We were still basking in the glow days afterwards however weeks later the anti-climax had hit and the realities of life had set in. The most significant thing after our wedding was the process of going back to work. I felt like a grown-up. The responsibility to my now complete family had set in. It was still exciting but a little frightening as well. For both of us I guess.

My post-wedding satisfaction level was a 5 because the buzz of the wedding had worn off and I was not working as yet. I had just moved to a new country and I was still adjusting. There was a time when I really felt unsure about the direction that I was going in. I had to rely on the belief that I had made the right decision by following my heart.

I feel that the post-wedding slump is both a physical and emotional thing. Wedding planning and events involve a lot of adrenaline that we almost become addicted to. Afterwards we experience withdrawal and crash. The emotional part is all the attention from your spouse, your family and friends. When everyone goes back to their daily routines we miss the constant expressions of love.

I experienced it a little. I was hesitant to get back to daily life. It seemed boring and I kept looking for ways to prolong the excitement. Nothing seemed to do the trick. I just had to take each day at a time until my motivation returned.

What has been tough since being married is realising that even though we are partners we will not always have the same priorities and desires. You still end up alone sometimes… and that is okay.

I also found it difficult to maintain my individuality both when it came to my opinions as well as my activities. My activities were always with him because I was new to the area and therefore hesitant about stepping out on my own. It was also expected by friends and family that we always agreed… so his opinions were expected to be mine.

I am most proud of the man that I married and that although we have gone through the growing pains of a young marriage we continue to love each other. We are equally committed to making this work.

Fariba, UK

How active were you in your career/business/career development before the wedding?

I'm full-time at HEFCE, the Higher Education Funding Council for England, working as a Policy Adviser in Equality and Diversity. Basically, I advise the university sector on equal opportunities issues such as the lack of disabled students accessing higher education, the low numbers of female professors compared to male and the high numbers of Black students concentrated at predominantly former polytechnic colleges and not Russell Group universities. It's quite varied and I like that there is no other person at HEFCE or elsewhere who does what I do. I get to schmooze with the bigwigs and get handed quite a lot of responsibility. Plus, it's interesting and I feel it feeds my soul as well as my head because I am passionate about the issues I'm working on.

I like my job and it is quite varied but I'm always looking for that next challenge or step up, particularly salary-wise. The thing is, I guess in 2008 when my (then) boyfriend proposed, I was still feeling challenged enough in the post to feel that I was at the right level. I only joined the organisation in April 2008 so had only been there for nine months! It was quite a big leap from where I was before in terms of salary, responsibility, independence so I was pleased to be in the position.

Before my engagement I was a 9/10 on a scale of life satisfaction (incorporating career considerations).

How did you find the wedding planning process?

Well, it was okay but tough, relationship wise. I remember my sister telling me that planning the wedding is a bit like an early glimpse (concentrated into a few months) of what married life will be like. It was. Dealing with all sorts of family politics, demands, money issues, learning to compromise, to talk calmly about stuff that seemed so important at the time like our colours for the event! Everything gets magnified and, looking back, we could have used some perspective. We learned a great deal about each other and probably went ten steps ahead in our relationship in the short period we were engaged than we did over the first six years. Because we're both so different but opinionated, discussions often ended in arguments so instead of having it take over our lives, we planned meetings at the end of each week to have a two hour slot where we would just hash out two or three details instead of talking about it every single day. That's what I remember about it, it just takes over and it seems that's all you can talk about! And when you're engaged for a year and a half, that's a long time to talk about one thing!

Compromising on the plans was one of the hardest lessons I've had to learn with my husband... And we're now putting those lessons to the test with our daughter!

How far do you agree with the statement... when I was planning my wedding, I focused less on my career development than I otherwise would have?

Strongly agree!

I wasn't interested in much else besides my wedding as trying to focus on anything else seemed like I was loading my plate. That said, I did start my LLM masters in human rights law... but my heart was definitely elsewhere.

My career satisfaction just after the wedding was a 6/10 – I just hadn't been focusing on career [progression] at all throughout the planning process. My job became a vehicle through which I could pay for our wedding! However, by the time we actually got married, so much time had passed, I naturally started to think about the next logical step. Two years in a post is probably enough time to start to feel comfortable and at least start thinking about moving on.

In my opinion, the post-wedding blues/post-wedding slump is realising that the high of planning one of the biggest days of your life is over, that all the energy, time, motivation, emotion that went into planning that one event has reached a climax and now it's over and now you have no outlet for it all. What do you do with all that time, emotion, and energy you invested now? What is the next big focus?

I actually missed this post-wedding slump in

motivation because we discovered we were pregnant nine days after returning from our honeymoon! It meant that we WERE able to move onto the next big project/focus. It meant that there was no slump because expecting a baby was just as exciting, just as consuming. I know I would have felt it hard though if we had had a break because we knew we wanted to try for one so the post-wedding slump combined with the waiting to get pregnant would have driven me crazy! Saying that, the shock of moving onto something so big was very overwhelming and we stayed mum for quite a while, while we tried to get our heads around the idea. I think there is such a thing as too much too soon! We dealt with it but it felt VERY overwhelming at the time!

What has been tough for you since getting married?

I guess realising that we are now a unit and have to think as one. I've always been used to being in complete control of everything I do, everything I buy, every decision I make – even after serious dating for six years, that's still how I thought. I think marriage brought it home that we had made a deep commitment and that every decision I made on my own had an equal effect on my husband. Buying or renting, quitting my job or moving somewhere else to take a job, all of this would be stuff we'd have to decide together. Heck, even just decorating our flat was a big deal! It really did feel different but was so great at the same time because I knew that's how he felt about me as well.

Since getting married I am most proud of our

relationship! I love being married. I love calling him my husband. We had a real extended honeymoon for nine months after our wedding, we were so excited! Our wedding was everything we could have ever asked for but the next few months felt just as exciting because we both just felt so content – like everything in our lives was in line.

How good are you at balancing time for yourself and time for being together?

Circumstances at the moment are a bit difficult because we have a newborn so I would say, not great. In fact, we haven't had any real time on our own since our baby was born eight months ago! But, slowly, she will be sleeping from 7–7 hopefully – giving us our evenings together. A pinched budget as we pay off a small loan we got to pay for the wedding and to pay for childcare also means we don't get to go out as much as we used to. We're not great at making quality time together, just time, which is something we need to work on.

Helen, Canada

How active were you in your career/business/career development before the wedding?

The year we got married, I moved back to Canada from the UK. I landed a full-time job at a magazine about six months before we got married, so the career was developing full-steam ahead.

Before our engagement, I'd say I was a 7/10 on a scale of satisfaction with life (incorporating areas of career). Our careers were both developing decently well before our engagement, but we had a long-distance relationship that year. Paul was working in the US and I was working in London when we got engaged. Not ideal! We knew there were a lot of changes ahead.

How did you find the wedding planning process?

I found it fairly straightforward in the beginning, there were several steps that you do early on (booking venue, etc.) that are easy. The difficult and challenging things come later – all of the detail-oriented tasks are stressful. Getting the invites out, decorations, place settings, flowers, making sure it's all done right.

During the process, I think I was fine except for three specific days: 1) we got lost on the way to a tasting at the caterers for the first time, and I had a mini-meltdown; 2) the store I ordered the bridesmaids dresses went out of business before they delivered them, so we had to (quickly) order them from another store a few months prior to the wedding; and 3) the night before the wedding, I was sure that I'd not decorated the venue enough.

How did you feel in the days and weeks following your wedding and honeymoon (i.e., when the wedding was officially over)?

It's very hard not to be 'The Bride' anymore – with everyone fussing over you and calling to discuss wedding details. When your special day is over, it's a bit deflating – until you remember the real reason why you got married! When you can look ahead to your life with your husband and all the great things that are still to come, it helps make that post-wedding deflated feeling slowly disappear.

I'm responding to these questions five years after getting married, so it was a while ago but I think the first significant thing that I did on return from honeymoon that was not wedding related was returning to work right after. It felt anticlimactic!

Since getting married, career change-wise, I started my own freelance writing business. Life-wise, we moved cities, bought a house and got a dog!

Sharmeen, USA

How active were you in your career/business/career development before the wedding?

I work full-time as a project coordinator at a large university, make-up artist part-time and I try to volunteer in a non-profit organisation a couple times a month (and more if I can). Before my engagement, I was a 4–5 on a career satisfaction scale because I wanted to do more than administrative work.

I STRONGLY AGREE that when I was planning my wedding, I focused less on my career development than I otherwise would have. In fact, the wedding is mostly all I focused on because I had time for nothing else. Also my lease for my apartment had ended and I was commuting from my parents' house to work (about a two hour drive each way with traffic – an hour without – sometimes more) and also trying to keep a gym/health routine.

How did you feel in the days and weeks following your wedding and honeymoon (i.e., when the wedding was officially over)?

Good that the overwhelming part was over. I felt ups and downs. A part of me just thought "is this it?" maybe I put too much expectation into how the marriage would be (I think our society does). I just felt upset over little things and felt that maybe he doesn't love me like I thought if he didn't want to cuddle. I was definitely making mountains out of molehills at times. It affected me the most when there was a physical lack of response. Not necessarily bad because I admit I am a little sensitive and I'm trying to work on that. But some of my husband's habits differ a lot from mine (he likes to watch TV almost every night, me not so much) and we disagreed on some principles – so in the very early days I felt like maybe the marriage wouldn't last.

I didn't want to share a lot of this with my husband because I thought he was going to think I am just insecure and not be interested in me anymore. It did not help at all, someone I know pretty well who had gotten married around the time I got engaged, was getting a divorce around the time I was getting married. So it just made me rethink everything twice, even if I knew I shouldn't.

In the immediate months following the wedding, I was a 7/10 in terms of career as I needed and still need more from my career.

This is just not what I want to do, so I feel like if I do something I love I will feel happier overall. But one the other hand, money is not a big issue with this job as it might be with a job I love. The early days of marriage just were not as great as I thought it would be. Also, I thought we would just be so lovey dovey and life would be a little more like a fairytale. I need a snap back to reality and at times it is, but not everyone is very lovey dovey ALL THE TIME, especially most men. Lastly, we were supposed to move and I wanted a physical change of scene but when that didn't happen, I felt like life wasn't moving forward like I needed it to.

My experience of the post-wedding blues/post-wedding slump is that there is too much expectation of every- thing to be perfect after the wedding in our society. When that doesn't happen, it create these blues because you think you spent all this money and effort into this day, or event and now you are married and it's like… now what? If there was more support and respect for reality, these issues would not be happening.

So what is the magic formula?

"The big secret in life is that there is no big secret. Whatever your goal, you can get there if you're willing to work."

Oprah Winfrey

The lesson I took away from these very personal experi- ences that brides throughout the world have generously shared is that there is no magic formula. Every single couple is different. How you feel is different to how someone else will feel and what works for one couple may not work for you. However, with this large variation in circumstance and experience, hopefully you have been inspired with some real examples of what does (and doesn't) work for couples in their quest for career/life balance – and everything in between.

Your values and beliefs

> *Your beliefs become your thoughts,*
> *Your thoughts become your words,*
> *Your words become your actions,*
> *Your actions become your habits,*
> *Your habits become your values,*
> *Your values become your destiny.*

> —Mohandas Gandhi

You have a set of values… what do they include? Collaboration, honesty, integrity, family? Freedom. Adventure, success? Are your values and beliefs a marriage made in heaven when it comes to your career – do your values match those of the company you are working for/your employer. Have your values and priorities changed since getting married?

Establishing your values and beliefs is an essential part of the path to career satisfaction and therefore an integral part of your career audit – regardless of whether or not you are a newlywed. If you haven't taken the time to establish your values however, it's not too late. This is a great time to start.

Laura Whitworth, Karen Kimsey-House and the varying authors of *Co-Active Coaching,* have an excellent definition of values. They say:

Values are not morals. There is no sense of morally right or wrong behaviour here. Values are not about moral character or ethical behaviour, though living in a highly ethical way may be a value. Values are not principles either, like self-government or standards of behaviour. Values are the qualities of a life lived fully from the inside out.

It is also emphasised that when we honour our values, we feel an internal 'rightness' and it is actually for this reason that giving yourself the time and space to establish your values and beliefs is a significant part of the career assessment and development process.

Imagine that. Imagine experiencing the harmony and satisfaction that comes as a result of our values matching our career ambitions. It is the matching/reunion of our values with our career that goes a long way to creating a happy working life.

If you are asking yourself how understanding your values can relate to your level of career/job satisfaction – think about the last time you were either very happy or alternatively, somewhat miserable in your role. Have you ever found that you are:

- Impressed by the open door/accessible policy of some of the most senior members of the business?
- Appreciative that your company is very involved in the community, with a solid understanding of their corporate social responsibility (CSR)? (For

instance, have you either fundraised for a charity or had half a day out of the office to paint a school or community area?)

- Pleased at the sense of teamwork (the 'we are all in this together' attitude) when a group of you have a really late night at the office?

- Proud to be praised and recognised for the good work that you do?

- Impressed (or not impressed) by your organisation's dedication to mentoring and supporting new staff, and their level of loyalty to the staff population in general?

- In the company of people who say "good morning", address each other by name and genuinely care about what each other is doing on the weekend/how their families are etc.?

- Disappointed that your organisation does not have a good health benefits package in place – factoring in discounted gym memberships and health insurance?

- Pleased/frustrated about staff opportunities to share their opinions for improving the business/ giving feedback?

- A fan of the more relaxed culture of drinks and snacks in the office on a Friday afternoon?

If any of these scenarios within organisations highlight something that you have had an opinion on, whether in a good or a bad way, it suggests that you have certain values (of fun, excellence, recognition etc.) that your company is or is not matching.

While it's unwise to expect that a company has an

ethos that completely matches your values (unless you started the company), we tend to be happiest in our work place when the values and vision of the company are congruent with ours. *This* is why understanding our values can contribute to our career satisfaction.

To do the values and beliefs discovery exercise below, it is important that you truly understand what constitutes a value. The *Co-Active Coaching* team explain:

> *They [values] are not something you do or have.*
> *Money for example is not a value, although money*
> *as a resource could lead to honouring values such as*
> *fun, creativity, achievement, peace of mind, service to*
> *others. Travel is not a value. Gardening is not a value.*
> *But both are examples of cherished activities that*
> *honour values including adventure, learning, nature,*
> *spirituality. And yet, although values are intangible,*
> *they are not invisible to others. You can walk into a*
> *room of strangers and get a sense of what people value*
> *by what they wear, how they stand in the room, how*
> *and with whom they interact, and the topics of their*
> *conversations. You can sense the values in the room:*
> *power, friendship, intimacy, connection, independence,*
> *fun and more.*

I will never forget the significant point in my career when I realised a company I was working for had values that didn't resonate with mine. Although I enjoyed some of my role, I diagnosed that the organisation's values and mine were in stark contrast. What did I do? I took about ten months of active job hunting to find a role that truly excited me and seemed to match my newly clarified values, thanked them for the great opportunity to work with them, wished them well and moved on to my new position with no hard feelings. I am still in touch with a number of colleagues from that organisation – and am confident that the move was one of the best career decisions I have made.

Observe your values to build the career you want.

Business coach Karen Williams agrees that when doing a career audit, it is important for a newlywed to make sure that they consider their values and beliefs in the process of assessing the current state of their career. She describes her own experience:

I left my job after my wedding as my values were no longer reflected in the role I was doing. So knowing your values is essential, especially as you don't want to go from the frying pan into the fire with regards to a job change. Don't make a rash decision and even if you don't like your job, it doesn't mean that you have to quit before you find something else. You also might want to think about the longer term as if you wish to have children, it may be more sensible to stay where you are.

Beliefs are slightly different. Having a strong self-belief and confidence are essential to a successful career change. A way of being sure of yourself is by being very clear on your strengths and transferable skills, and the type of work where you will excel.

Career Audit Exercise 2:
Establish your values

Which of the following values resonate with you?
Underline all of those which highlight your own
values (and/or add your own). Then number the top
five, putting yourself in the best possible position to be
informed and considered in your career development:

Excellence	Stability	Achievement	Contributing to a cause
Fun	Support	Self-respect	Truth
Adventure	Accountability	Teamwork	Marriage
Partnership	Justice	Friendship	Extravagance
Ethics	Discipline	Commitment	Connection
Diversity	Approachability	Enthusiasm	Independence

Additional values: _____

_____

Your beliefs

*"What we can or cannot do, what we consider possible or
impossible, is rarely a function of our true capability. It is
more likely a function of our beliefs about who we are."*

Tony Robbins

Establishing your values is a key ingredient in achieving your own personal career success (whatever that looks
like to you), however it is important to assess the beliefs
you have surrounding what you think you are capable of.

Beliefs are:
- A state of mind in which trust or confidence is placed in some person or thing
- Conviction of the truth of some statement or the reality of some being or phenomenon, especially when based on examination of evidence
- The ideas you support and have a commitment to
- The views and opinions that you have accumulated, that represent you.

"Beliefs have the power to create and the power to destroy. Human beings have the awesome ability to take any experience of their lives and create a meaning that disempowers them or one that can literally save their lives.

Tony Robbins

Your beliefs emerge in the actions you take and the words you use. Your confidence or lack of confidence in certain areas can also be a result of your beliefs. Think about it… you may believe that everyone will look at you strangely if you walk into a social situation alone so you refuse to do so. You may believe that you can do anything you set your mind to. Or, you may believe that a certain task is impossible, and therefore not try particularly hard. Your beliefs are extremely powerful and it is worth taking the time to be aware of what beliefs you have and are displaying.

Do you believe your boss is scary? Do you believe someone you know is superior or inferior to you? What beliefs do you have that do not serve you well when it comes to your aspirations? Whatever your beliefs are,

Career Audit Exercise 3:
Challenge your beliefs

What three beliefs do I have which may be detrimental
to me in achieving the career success I seek?

1. _____
   _____
   _____

2. _____
   _____
   _____

3. _____
   _____
   _____

What actions can I take to turn the beliefs above into
something more positive? Or, what belief do I choose
to adopt instead of the above?

4. _____
   _____
   _____

5. _____
   _____
   _____

6. _____
   _____
   _____

they manifest in your behaviour and they can affect your career prospects. So, be aware of what they are and either use them as they are to your advantage, or work to change them if they aren't serving a positive purpose for you.

"If you don't change your beliefs, your life will be like this forever. Is that good news?"

W. Somerset Maugham

Your career: next steps

You've just undertaken a career audit earlier in this chapter, including the process of establishing your values and beliefs. Now, for the first time since before your engagement (or for the first time ever in some cases!) you may have made some major, calculated decisions about your career direction.

The next section of this chapter gives you support to achieve those new career goals. There are top tips and shared advice in the areas of how to approach your boss for a promotion or pay rise if you're happy where you are in your current role and looking for the next opportunity in your company. And there are tips for job hunting in any market if you think the best option for you is to move onto a new job or start exploring a new career. Finally, there are some unusual interview tips (for when you start the process) and information about where you can seek support for all of the above.

Please note: the information below does not constitute a one size fits all formula but highlights some approaches which have worked in my experience of career coaching and which you can consider if you are at this stage.

How to approach your boss about a promotion

"If you don't go after what you want, you'll never have it. If you don't ask, the answer is always no. If you don't step forward, you're always in the same place."

Nora Roberts

You have done your career audit and decided that you are happy with your current employer. That's great... chances are, you would therefore like your next phase of career development to take place where you are currently working.

If you think you are nearly (but not quite) ready for the promotion you seek, take the time to ensure you are doing your job well. It is important to dot the i's and cross the t's... detail is key. Review what you do well in reference to your job description and start working towards what you can be doing even better. That way, you can be confident of the contribution you are making when it comes to speaking to your boss about next steps.

"Plenty of men can do good work for a spurt and with immediate promotion in mind, but for promotion you want a man in whom good work has become a habit."

Henry L Doherty

If you feel that you are already working at the level where a promotion should be imminent (or should have already happened!), here are some steps for you to consider when approaching your boss about promotion or a pay rise:

Step 1: Find your original job description and compare your progress between then and now regarding tasks expected of you as part of the role

If you are seeking to move up to the next level, it is important to be able to highlight in tangible terms that you are not only meeting but you are far exceeding the requirements of your current position. Remember, promotions tend to be given to the person who is already working at the next level as opposed to those who may be capable but have not yet proved they can do so.

Step 2: Prepare for your annual appraisal/propose your own career development meeting

Do not feel compelled to wait for your next annual/ biannual appraisal. If you are serious about achieving promotion you can show how serious you are by proposing a meeting to discuss your job role/career progress with your manager. This is a meeting where you set the agenda and make it clear that you would like to progress through the ranks of the organisation.

Be clear about what promotion means for you. Is it a move within your department? A change of job title? An increase in salary? An increase of responsibility/a greater choice of projects within the workplace? All of the above? Understand what it is you really want so you can communicate it clearly.

Where possible, compile some testimonials in relation to your work. This may be emails from colleagues or comments on your LinkedIn profile. These endorsements of your abilities will be a great reflection of the points you are making.

Outline some of the above in a pre-meeting email to your boss so they understand what the meeting is about and can start to turn their thinking towards what you want to discuss.

Step 3: Make the most of the meeting

Highlight – with tangible numbers and clear examples where possible – the success achieved within your current role. Make your ambitions clear, but also get across your passion and desire to stay within the company as your career develops.

Make it clear that you are ready and feel that you have achieved enough for that to be recognised formally, through achieving promotion.

In an ideal world, promotion would be agreed then and there. However, in the absence of a looming official appraisal meeting, it is unlikely that your manager has been thinking of your next promotion unprompted. Perhaps most likely, this is the beginning of a clear and mutually agreed process of what needs to be done for you to get there.

Set time frames (which you propose); set clear objectives and book in your next review meeting then and there (to take place in three months for example).

Step 4: Follow up verbal discussions in writing

Within a week of the meeting, confirm the discussions you had and the agreements made in writing. Also include some of those testimonials you secured (where relevant). What are the specific areas where you need to re-emphasise your abilities? This does not necessarily need to be more detailed than a solid, well thought out email with bullet point actions, but the follow up in writing further highlights how serious you are about this.

Step 5: Be bold, be patient, be persistent

Achieving your goal of a promotion may not happen overnight but by following the steps above, you have opened a productive and dynamic dialogue about your future with the company.

"There are two kinds of people, those who do the work and those who take the credit. Try to be in the first group; there is less competition there."

Indira Gandhi

You have highlighted the many positive aspects of your achievement for the business in real terms and you have listened to your manager about what they think you need to achieve to reach the next level. Even if you think you are already at the level required, don't get frustrated. Take heart from the fact that the initiative you have taken means you have removed any ambiguity from the situation and you are now working to a clear and mutually agreed set of objectives.

Work towards these and meticulously continue to keep records of praise received and achievements made. Aided by these steps, you should hopefully be well on your way to achieving that promotion.

Top tips for job hunting in any market

"Believe in yourself and all that you are. Know that there is something inside you that is greater than any obstacle."

Christian D. Larson

"The world of achievement has always belonged to the optimist."

Harold Wilkins

If your post-wedding career audit has made you realise that you no longer want to be in your current job or work for your current company, it means that job hunting is on the cards (unless you decide to start your own business).

That means you may be job hunting in a time of recession or in a time of prosperity. Whatever the economy, there are still opportunities available to the right candidates, you just need to know where to look to find them.

Each of the steps set out below could be a chapter in its own right (hopefully another book, another time). But for now, have a look at some of these tips and act on the ones that resonate with you.

1.   *Re-create your CV:*
     That's right. Re-create. Don't update or tweak, unless you have given your CV a complete makeover recently. While the majority of the information will move over to the new one, it is a good idea to start from scratch in a format that feels like it represents you today.

2.   *Follow the news in the industry you are aspiring to become a part of:*

Get to know what is happening in your chosen industry. And remember, the fact that you are currently working in your field does not automatically mean that you are up to date on current trends. Regardless of whether you are changing industries or not, take the time to truly get a grasp of what is going on. Read the business pages, explore trade-specific websites and follow leading organisations within that industry. Look at their news pages. Consistently keeping up to date will give you the confidence needed to feel like a great candidate for the roles you come across.

3.   *Identify the best general and industry-specific websites for you*

I remember a period when it felt like *The Guardian* jobs website was frequented more than Facebook, Twitter or any of my regular favourites. Seek the best general site for you and the best industry-specific ones. Register and specify the parameters of the jobs you are looking for in order to receive daily email alerts to aid your search.

4.   *Tell people you are job hunting*

This may not be an obvious one but it can be extremely beneficial. Clearly, you *need to be* selective in who you tell. Telling your manager or current colleagues is not advisable. However if you have friends/acquaintances that you trust

implicitly, then let them know that you are looking for your next opportunity and what type of
thing you would like to be doing. People hear
about opportunities on a daily basis in their own
workplaces and via friends, and if they know
that you are looking, they can let you know of
anything relevant they come across. If they don't
know – you wouldn't come to mind.

5.   *Create a good LinkedIn profile:*
LinkedIn is the social networking site for professionals. If you don't yet have a presence on
LinkedIn – this is the time to start. Seriously,
step away from the book (briefly) and create
your profile now. If you are on the site but your
profile is incomplete, take the time to complete
it. Again, step away momentarily from the book
– just do it. LinkedIn is an efficient use of time
and effort for today's job seeker because not only
do you connect with people you know professionally (including ex-colleagues, clients, school
and university friends and more), but you create
an online CV which is visible to these connections and to employers alike. You can join
groups which reflect your business interests and
people can write testimonials about your work
(in your current and in previous roles). A recent
update means that people can endorse you for
skills you've listed on your profile. It's a dynamic
way to put yourself in the job market. There are
countless benefits of LinkedIn and if the above
hasn't convinced you, do a search on Google

on the importance of LinkedIn for job seekers. Convinced ? Good. Sort out your profile now.

6.   *Get onto Twitter*

While the benefits of LinkedIn are well known to many professionals, the benefits of Twitter are less apparent and jobseekers do not take advantage of this social networking site in the way they could. The impression of many non-Twitter users is that the site is a place where people fritter away time unnecessarily. Some think of it as a passing fad. What I am happy to confirm is that if you follow the right people and organisations on Twitter, it is one of the most effective job-seeking tools available today.

Twitter is a place where people love to connect and share. So it would be remiss of you not to join and follow the organisations, businesses and people who are of interest to you professionally. There, you often hear about jobs and volunteer opportunities first and you have the opportunity to follow industry leaders who freely share their thoughts and movements with you. From their thoughts about *The X Factor* to any business initiatives and competitions they run, as well as roles available – you become part of an audience who has direct access to this useful source.

To take it a step further, if you want to understand more about what the employer or industry leader is interested in, look at who they follow and you can follow those you consider relevant in terms of your job hunt. There are many benefits of Twitter for job seekers. If you don't actively and decisively take advantage of this medium, you risk joining the mass of job hunters who are not using all of the tools at their disposal.

7.   *Ignore the doom and gloom*
It isn't advisable to pretend the world's economic challenges do not exist, but it is encouraging to remember that you are your own person who can take the actions required to stand out in a crowded job market. As with everything else, job hunting can be a self-fulfilling prophecy. If you can only see the difficulties, you are less likely to be as successful as you should be with your hunt. However, if you keep current, are flexible, positive, resourceful and use the various tools at your disposal – it will hopefully soon be time to celebrate your new opportunity. Good luck!

"Learn how to be happy with what you have while you pursue all that you want."

Jim Rohn

Career Audit Exercise 4:
Start on your professional social networking journey

Set up your LinkedIn and Twitter accounts as explained above. Step out of your comfort zone. Using these mediums correctly will improve your job-seeking prospects so don't hesitate.

Unusual interview tips

"It's not who you are that holds you back,
it's who you think you're not."

Author Unknown

At some stage, your job search will involve an interview —or many! Below are some tips for interview success that you may not have heard. I initially wrote this article for publication in *The Voice*, a British newspaper but I have reprinted it below as it may be useful for you in your career journey.

Secrets of effective job hunting

FIRSTLY, CONGRATS on getting to interview stage. Your application has stood out against countless others, now it's just about making that connection in person. Nerves may very much be coming into play here, which is natural – but by considering the below, you may be putting yourself ahead of the pack, by doing something a little bit different to other candidates.

TIP 1: Social intelligence

Remember, interviews are all about getting to know you better, ultimately working out if you connect with the business and your potential new boss. Research by CareerBuilder.co.uk has shown that 53% of employers research candidates online – including on social networks like Facebook and LinkedIn. Why should they have all the fun? You should be doing the same thing, not in attempt to catch anyone out – but in an attempt to get to know more about your interviewer. Remember, your upcoming interview is your chance to make a potential connection with the interviewer, so if you have any common ground, maximise on it.

Here's what you do:

1.   Make sure you get the names of your interviewers when the company calls or emails to tell you the good news of your interview – this is essential.

2.   Check out their profiles online (both business and personal). This intelligence may be useful. If you find out that they are a competitive horse-back rider and this was one of your favourite hobbies when you were younger, you can mention that winning a medal at a competition is one of your proudest life moments (for example). If they have a full LinkedIn profile, you can also find out how long they've been at their current company and where they worked previously and if you have any similarities here, use that information as a way of connecting.

3.   This may be stating the obvious, but it's all about using this intelligence sensibly. If Facebook told you that they had a 'big night' over the weekend, it is not your place to ask 'how they're feeling' if they have 'recovered' – no matter how friendly you can make that sound. Save that banter for when you get the job (if it's that kind of work environment).

TIP 2: Show and tell

If a picture is worth a thousand words, then a demonstration of your claims may be worth a million. Regardless of what position you are going for, you can prepare a top three list of the things you would be keen to explore if you were to be offered the position. This could be an implementation from scratch or an increase of what's already being done.

Remember – your mission is NOT to claim that you know better than current employees (that may irk your interviewer), but to highlight that you've done enough research to have a clear idea of what you can really bring to the table. You can create this in a one-page proposal form, including a SWOT analysis (strengths, weaknesses, opportunities and threats) if you really want to go to town on it. This is a move which will clearly indicate that you have the ability to do what you claim you can do.

In interviews, remember not to forget any relevant work experience you have had which can demonstrate the skills you need for the job you are going for.

TIP 3: Fool yourself out of your nerves!

Still worried that your nerves mean that you may hinder the opportunity you have? Here's an item you must take to your interview – however, this one is for your eyes only. This may involve a bit of a treasure hunt at home, but for this tactic, you need to find an item which never ceases to make you smile.

From a silly photo of you and some friends to a comic book you used to love as a child. Or a birthday card with hilarious cover art to a LinkedIn recommendation that you're proud of. Maybe even something like a print-out of the ridiculous lyrics of a catchy song or an image of your favourite meal. Make this object the last thing you look at before being called into your interview. Chances are, you'll meet your interviewer wearing a very real, sparkly smile – ensuring you make a dazzling first impression.

In considering adopting these tactics, bear in mind that they are an enhancement, not a substitute, for traditional interview tips such as preparing questions to ask your interviewer (a must!) and being well presented. But they are designed to give you the edge by making you stand out in a positive way.

Further career development support

"Anyone who has achieved excellence in any form knows that it comes as a result of ceaseless concentration."

Louise Brooks

The area of career satisfaction can be tricky generally. However, for women in particular, and for newlyweds, new parents or anyone who has been focusing on something or someone deemed more significant for a period of time, it is especially important to take the time to assess where you currently are on your career journey and work out where you want to be.

Along your journey, take advantage of the support you have available to you. This may be in the form of people you know personally, like family and friends, or people you know professionally, like mentors or coaches. Seek out the support that will help you achieve your career goals in the most effective way you can. Don't feel you necessarily have to do everything on your own – including keeping up the motivation.

By reading, participating in the exercises and acting on any top tips that resonated with you in this chapter you should now have a better sense of:

- Your values and beliefs
- How to approach your boss about promotion/a pay rise
- How to prepare for your annual appraisal/propose your own career development meeting
- Top tips for job hunting in any market (including using Twitter and LinkedIn)
- Unusual interview tips
- The kind of support available in your bid to make positive steps in developing your career (a mentor, coach etc).

"Every day I get up and look through the Forbes list of the richest people in America. If I'm not there, I go to work."

Robert Orben

Good luck shaping you career into what you want it to be. Be strong, know your strengths, be confident in your abilities… and bring it!

Chapter **7**

Love, Laugh and communicate: Set your own rules of communication

"The single biggest problem with communication is the illusion that it has taken place."

George Bernard Shaw

You don't have to be a relationship expert, psychologist or communications guru to realise that effective communication is at the heart of any authentically good relationship. It is the lack of communication which can lead to countless disappointments and perpetual heartbreak – while consistent communication can result in smoother sailing along the journey. This is true of a parent and child, business manager and employee, between friends – and it is certainly true of husband and wife.

Understanding the value of communication in relationships for every couple – and what your own particular set of communications rules are – is an essential step towards a happy and successful marriage and towards moving on from the post-wedding blues.

This importance isn't new. Although in this era where there are vastly increased platforms for communication, the importance of solid communication as a couple and the need to set your own rules of communication is heightened. With the advent of social media, it is not only traditional communication you need to consider but also the effect that technology can have on your relationship.

In this chapter, you will gain greater insight into:

- Three top tips highlighting how effective communication within a relationship helps in achieving both personal and professional satisfaction
- How to share goals and daily/weekly accomplishment celebrations
- How to have a stake in each other's career goals (share the boring details of work, the project you are working on, proposals to be done)
- The new communication rules thanks to new media.

Three top tips for effective communication during the early days of marriage

"Assumptions are the termites of relationships."

Henry Winkler

This short but powerful quote from Henry Winkler stresses why effective communication is so important in relationships. Assumptions are dangerous and can eat away at what you are trying to build. This is especially important to remember as human nature lends itself to assumption. Without the facts and solid communication levels to avoid falling prey to them, assumptions can be detrimental to a relationship and a barrier to the goals of the individuals within that relationship.

Imagine, for example, that two members of the same couple both assumed that the other partner would be the one to make more significant compromises in their career to accommodate the career progress of the other. Imagine that. It isn't too difficult is it? That is exactly the kind of scenario that a couple comprising two career-driven individuals may find themselves in if they do not communicate clearly about their career plans and lifestyle desires.

With that in mind, and in no particular order of importance, addressing the five areas below may prove beneficial in the early days of marriage, and should continue to be just as valuable as marriage progresses.

Tip 1: Drown out the noise: be patient and listen to each other

At our wedding, my father said to my husband and me what is possibly one of the most profound things I had heard in relation to marriage. He said "Remember, the two of you are now family… we are your relatives. Your dedication is to each other, although we are here to support you both whenever needed."

He went on to explain his words in more detail, highlighting the idea that *relatives* are those among whom we find ourselves; the social milieu we were born into – parents, siblings, aunts, uncles, close friends of your parents etc. "You are part of the family, but it is not your family." *Family* is what you create, spouse and offspring – including any adopted or step-children.

Those words meant a lot to us. While we have no

intention of suddenly ignoring the parents and families we have always known and loved – the sentiment that we were now each other's priorities was an important one, which resonated with us.

What my dad was referring to in stressing this new priority was some of that 'noise' that a couple may sometimes let affect them – a parent's opinion, a sibling's interpretation and more. While friends and family will always be significant in your lives, no one can truly understand a couple but the couple themselves. So sometimes, the (unsolicited) two cents worth from a party external to your relationship needs to remain on the periphery.

Furthermore, a key part of drowning out the noise is to continually strengthen the trust that you hold as a pair. Having already emphatically condemned assumptions, I won't assume, but I would sincerely hope that you did not marry someone you were unsure about trusting. While burying your head in the sand is unwise, it is worth remembering that your default should be to trust your partner. If that's broken, you deal with that break in trust at the time, but it is advisable to start at a level where you first defend instead of accuse.

Tip 1b: Fun ways to drown out the noise!

While the lyrics to the 2006 song entitled *Listen*, (written by Henry Krieger, Scott Cutler, Anne Preven, and Beyoncé Knowles and sung by Beyoncé), are a reflection of a couple at the end of their time together – 'Listen' is a word that my husband and I half-jokingly (and half-seriously!) sing to each other – on the occasions when we want to remind the other to listen to the point being made.

While the context surrounding this song is of a fed up, desperate woman, about to leave her husband – yes, it's that dramatic – jokingly singing the title word is one of the (many) ways R and I make sure we have each other's attention when communicating.

It doesn't matter what you do as a couple, but as long as you establish your own way to drown out the noise and have important conversations when necessary, you are onto a winner.

Further Reading & Listening

If you're curious, you can find a selection of the song's lyrics on a range of music lyric websites if you search "Beyonce" and "Listen". Alternatively, you can listen to the song on the Dreamgirls (2007) movie soundtrack or via YouTube.

Tip 2: Have fun together! Make date night a firm part of your schedule

"Our life before moving to Washington was filled with simple joys...Saturdays at soccer games, Sundays at grandma's house...and a date night for Barack and me was either dinner or a movie, because as an exhausted mom, I couldn't stay awake for both."

Michelle Obama

One of the main reasons for initially getting together with your spouse is that you have fun together – whatever fun may be to the two of you as a couple. Generally speaking, people form a partnership based on what they have in common and the fact that they enjoy each other's company. With that in mind, as life goes on and our varying priorities (work, children etc) fight for space in our lives, it becomes increasingly important to make a concerted effort to spend time together as a couple. Time together is the very foundation of anything that has since evolved.

Enter… 'Date night'

'Date night' is something that is so often recommended to couples that the notion may seem like a cliché. But this is an instance where it has become a cliché for a reason: because it is important, it is popular and it works.

In her *Strengthening Marriage* blog, Laura M. Brotherson, Marriage and Intimacy Expert, Author of *And They Were Not Ashamed--Strengthening Marriage through Sexual Fulfillment*, and founder of StrengtheningMarriage. com emphasises that:

> *One of the purposes of date night is to build positive associations of fun and enjoyment with your spouse and the relationship you share. It's just too easy for the weight of the world to pull you apart without dedicated time and attention for pleasurable reconnecting with your spouse. Don't let the opportunity pass you by!*

It is worth repeating Laura's advice: don't let the opportunity pass you by! Irrespective of whether both members of a couple are out of the house at work during the day or not, one of the best opportunities for a married couple to truly spend quality time together is through establishing a regular date night. This provides you with an opportunity to catch up with each other, with no distractions.

And it is the 'no distractions' which is key. If you're having dinner together at home, you will be more focused on your children, if you have a family. Or if you don't have kids, the focus may be on TV, your thoughts of an intense day at the office, a load of washing that needs doing or any other number of things that take away from your time to focus on each other and quality togetherness.

Enter date night: a night where a couple can get a babysitter if needed and enjoy each other's company over a meal, movie, debate, dance class, shared other hobby or any plethora of options.

Los Angeles based Erin Tillman, also known as 'The Dating Advice Girl' has some great tips.

> *Just because you are in a long-term relationship, doesn't mean that you can't keep it fresh! It can be easy to get stuck in a relationship rut when in a long-term partnership and get comfortable doing the same thing every night with your partner. That's when things get mundane and we get stuck in a rut. The idea of doing something new with your partner can immediately add a fun and exciting dynamic to your relationship date nights. As a dating expert, my goal is to help single people enjoy the dating process by helping them take control of their dating lives and suggesting fun date night ideas to keep dating fun, not daunting. I personally think that these same date night ideas and principles can be useful to long-term couples too. By planning a date night with your mate, you'll bring back those butterflies and reignite your original relationship spark. Small things like getting all dressed up,*

arranging to pick your partner up for your date, and exchanging small gifts of appreciation are all things that you can do to keep things fresh between you and your mate. In addition to that, here are a couple of date night ideas to keep things fun and lively.

Tip #1: Take a vacation in your city

You don't need to book an expensive exotic vacation to escape from the status quo. Why not plan a vacation in your own city? Planning a mini-getaway in your city is a practical and less expensive way to enjoy a change of scenery with your mate. Something as simple as booking a room at a nice hotel and dining at a new restaurant in your town could add a spark to your relationship ember without breaking the bank or traveling long distances.

Tip #2: Try a new activity together

Try a new activity that you've always wanted to try. Take a cooking class, learn how to paint or draw, or go big and go skydiving together! Participating in a new activity with your partner helps you to share and learn together. When you learn something new together, you automatically strengthen your bond by working as a team to create or share an exciting experience. Besides participating in a fun new activity, you will also always carry the satisfaction of you and your partner actively making each other's dreams come true.

One of the perks of a long-term relationship is the comfort factor, but if we get too comfortable in our relationships it can kill the flirtatiousness, sexiness and excitement of it all. Make it your relationship goal to have a proper date night on a regular basis with your partner. Do what you can to keep things fresh with your partner!

Further Reading & Listening

Francesca Di Meglio, a journalist who has written about weddings, marriage, sex, romance, parenting, and personal finance for numerous publications and websites has a number of ideas for date night. She shares 50 Great Date Ideas in the About.com Guide. You can read more here:
http://newlyweds.about.com/od/lovesex/a/datenights.htm

Erin and Francesca both have some great date ideas which will hopefully inspire you to plan some fun dates of your own. Remember, it becomes harder for the post-wedding blues to factor in your newlywed days when you are proactive about creating dates that will raise a giggle and strengthen your bond.

Tip 3: Share your successes and challenges

*The goal in marriage is not to think alike,
but to think together.*

Robert C. Dodds

One of the most effective ways to surpass any sense of post-wedding blues you may have, while strengthening your partnership, is to make a conscious effort to share your successes and challenges with each other.

"The friendship that we established early on in our marriage ... that carries you through tough times. That and a good sense of humour."

President Obama

While you may be bound together in matrimony by law, you are not joined at the hip and as a result you have a number of very different experiences and challenges to each other over the course of a day, week, month, or year.

Share those experiences. Share those challenges.

I am not suggesting that you ask your other half to come deal with the boss that is royally p***ing you off (although that may be tempting at times!) but I am recommending the tips below when setting your own rules of communication to truly strengthen your partnership.

To get you started with your rule setting, here are some you may want to consider incorporating:

1. Create an open forum to communicate the good, bad and ugly of your day

    This involves not just posing the question "How was your day?" but genuinely listening to the answer – having the conversation flow from there is a great start. Sometimes the routine of daily life can feel like a battle (whether it is the traffic conspiring against you or that colleague being a royal pain in the **** again!) and feeling like your spouse is part of your army, which strengthens your partnership through solid communication.

If it's difficult to set aside that time on a daily basis, you can hold that thought by keeping a jar on your kitchen counter (or bedside table) where you can both insert notes about a point/topic/ funny story you want to share. Just because you can't immediately share a moment doesn't mean you have to lose the moment, so do make the effort to share your daily experiences.

Share. Laugh out loud. Commiserate together. How can you be blue when you have this level of relationship with your other half?!

2. Communicate your individual and shared goals: keep a success journal

The topic of individual and joined goal setting was extensively covered earlier in the book, however it is worth mentioning again here since communicating and reinforcing these goals is an important step in strengthening your unity as a couple.

Take the time to fit 'big picture' thinking into your everyday existence where possible. The way to do this will very much depend on your daily routines and your ability to take advantage of the moments when you are together in the day.

As mentioned previously, one of the things that work for R and me is to discuss our goals for the day first thing in the morning when we're in the car on the way to the train station. We don't just ask "What are you up to today" but also ask each other things like "What needs to happen today for you to consider your day to be a successful one?" and "How are you going to tackle the task you are least looking forward to today?" That way, when it comes to our end of day catch up, we've got a solid basis for that discussion and can celebrate the small wins together.

In addition, because we're busy as lots of us tend to be, it is easy to just get through the day and survive – we also regularly take the time to write a success journal.

Keeping a success journal involves writing down your daily accomplishments and it's something which really works for us because we individually take five to ten minutes to write about what achievements we are proud of in that day and then read them to each other. These don't have to be anything ground breaking! It's not about only highlighting the big wins like securing a new client or gaining a promotion but it's also about celebrating any small wins in line with what your goals are. This might be choosing a salad instead of a burger or making a phone call and catching up with a family member you've been meaning to get in touch with.

Success journals are not a new idea. In fact, they are highly recommended as a personal or business performance tool. A Google search of "keep a success journal" yields over 83 million results – a testament to how widely spread this approach is.

If you hate the idea of spending days and months on end feeling unfulfilled because what you tend to remember is what you have not achieved – this is an approach you won't regret trying.

3.   Discuss and agree on your priorities

At the beginning of the book, I briefly mentioned *The Million Pound Drop*, a television game show which broadcasts in the UK on Channel 4. I promised I'd tell you more about how it fits into the story of R and me as a couple. This is the place to do it as it's quite an interesting (and perhaps unusual) example of how important it is for a couple to discuss and subsequently agree on their priorities.

Described as an extraordinary game show event, where contestants can win or lose life-changing amounts of money live on TV, *The Million Pound Drop* format involves contestants being given their prize at the top of the show – one million pounds in CASH – and all they have to do is keep hold of it:

Just eight questions stand between the contestants and their chance to take home the prize. This is played out on 'The Drop' – a fiendish device with four trapdoors, on which the answers to each question are displayed. Contestants place their money on the trapdoor they think displays the correct answer. They can spread the money across the trapdoors if they aren't sure. If the answer is wrong, the money they placed will fall through the doors to be lost forever. Just one wrong move could literally see thousands of pounds drop through the floor.

What   does   this   have   to   do   with   the

communications rule "discuss and agree on your priorities?"

Simple really – it's an example of a couple keeping their perspective and staying on the same page. You may remember R and I married on the same day as Prince William and Kate Middleton – and the nation and beyond had truly been gripped by wedding fever. It seems the producers of the show were no exception and they were looking for couples who were getting married that weekend to appear on the show! Our registrar gave them our details (with our consent) and on the week of our wedding, I had a number of conversations with a lovely producer on the show about what they were looking for. The opportunity to appear on the show and potentially win a decent sum of money to start our married life was an exciting one, but my heart dropped when I realised they would want us at the studio on the actual day of our wedding.

As it was such a fun opportunity, I even went so far as to discuss the logistics of what time we'd need to leave our wedding reception in Windsor (a town outside London) to get back to London for the filming and whether we could set up a screen so our reception guests could watch us on the show! However, when we realised we'd need to leave our own wedding celebrations soon after our ceremony, in discussions with R, we unanimously came to

Couples Communication Exercise 1:
Success journal prompts

If you have never kept a success journal before, you may benefit from a few prompts to help you work out what you can include in your journal. Ask yourself:

- What have I accomplished today?
- What really challenged me today and what did I do to overcome it?
- What decisions have I made today which get me closer to my goals?
- What made me smile today?
- What am I proud of today?

With the above in mind (or with appropriate prompts of your own), write your first success journal entry here:

1. _____

   _____

2. _____

   _____

3. _____

   _____

How did that feel? Imagine doing the exercise alongside your other half and sharing the things on that list.

Sound good? Good. Find (or go out and buy) a couple of notebooks so you can start the process together. It is a simple exercise which will help you highlight your many accomplishments (big and small) and is also a great communications tool for you as a couple.

the conclusion that the only place we wanted to be on that day was at our reception with our family and friends – even the lure of thousands of pounds wasn't going to detract us from that.

Set your own rules of communication! The most random, unforeseen opportunities (like this one) may come up in your lives and it's not the decision you make that counts – it is how you reach it that matters. If you reach an agreed conclusion together – based on shared priorities, you won't have any regrets.

[Note to any producers of the show who may be reading this book: Please feel free to invite us back if you ever have a royal wedding anniversary show!]

Communication challenges and triumphs of newlyweds

"My words fly up, my thoughts remain below: Words without thoughts, never to heaven go."

William Shakespeare, Hamlet. Act III. Sc. 3

A number of newlyweds shared their varying experiences with me in the research stages of this book, and the subject of communication was a topic that regularly featured – in a variety of contexts. See some of them below and reflect on whether this is something that you can envisage being applicable to you or maybe it already resonates with you.

What has been tough since getting married?

Trena:

Since I had been living alone for quite some time I was used to my space and having things organized a certain way. After getting married initially it was great when we were finally living together, but then one day it hit me.... I was like... oh wow he's here 24/7!! I missed my space and how neat and tidy my place was. That didn't last long though, through communication and compromise we work things out.

Pamela:

I think the things that have been tough have been taking on new responsibilities as a team, like getting and training our dog. We have gotten to know a bit more about each other's "parenting" styles, and that has definitely been a learning experience.

There are also adjustments that need to be made with families around holidays, visits, etc. that you have to adapt to now that you have a whole new family. We have been pretty successful at that, but it is a challenge sometimes with my family being 4 hours away and his being down the street.

Bianca:

Getting my head around the fact that his money and my money are the same. We don't need to be splitting everything down the middle as before. Especially as we were together for 6 years before we got engaged and 8 years before we got married - it's a weird one that I am not sure I totally understand even now. Is there even a correct way of thinking about it?

Carolina:

Realising that it is for life and a decision that is made every day... Deciding where to live!

Anita:

Nothing really! My hubby supports me in anything that I want to do. He is always there for and with me. Of course, there are some times when we may not totally agree on something but we work on that and come to a compromise. What helps too is that when we got married, we made a promise not to go to bed upset with each other and that has worked for us.

How good are you at balancing time for yourself and time for being together?

Stacy:

Could be better, especially when I have a deadline. Time for myself is often just working. I try to ensure we eat together in the evenings (we did so before we got married) and we attend about one joint social event per fortnight. I think I need to carve out more time for myself that isn't work related.

Elizabeth:

Since falling pregnant, I've spent more evenings at

home than I did previously so we've had a lot more
together time. I find that at the moment I want to
spend as much free time with my partner as possible,
though I still enjoy taking time for myself whether
that's being out and about with friends or hitting the
gym.

Julie:

Not so good at the moment but we allocate special
weekends which we cannot cancel on pain of death.
My husband has two children who visit each weekend
so we have to take that into account too. He also had
a new job to which he travels 120 miles each day. This
is not a sob story we are super happy but time is of the
essence and we are now quite strict about spending
it with each other. We miss our time very much – we
need to be out of the house to talk and not concentrate
on everyday bills, decorating etc.

Alex:

Same as before (being married), we make sure we
spend time with our friends and encourage each other
to do so. We always share our plans so we can try and
co-ordinate nights out and know where each other are.

Katy:

Unfortunately with work and money it's not often at
all we get just 'us time' but on the rare occasion we do
we make the most of it. As it's not on a regular basis it
makes it even more special when we do.

Salma:

I've never stopped in my tracks and thought 'Oh I don't spend enough time on my own,' as I'm not one of those people who needs that; I prefer to socialise. Every month Richard and I have at least one date out and weekly we make a point of cooking a really nice meal together. We have time with our friends and also Richard gets to play his computer games when I'm working on planning lessons at the weekend. I think we've got it worked out quite nicely to be honest!

Ida

Very good. I think that the best advice I've gotten for relationships was from my friend's pastor (when she was getting married): "You can't both be angry at once." That goes for any negative feelings. If one of you is angry/frustrated/upset/sad, the other one needs to balance that out, or you both get dragged down and it's completely unconstructive. You need to stay strong for the other one, be patient, stay calm, and ride through it together. You need to "allow" the other one's feelings. Once the strong feelings pass, you can talk/share/analyse it in a more calm, honest manner.

It's also VERY important to do your own individual things. You need to actually schedule in family time, friends time, hobbies time. If you depend too much on your partner for your needs (emotional/spiritual/sports/fun) it becomes stifling and frustrating for both of you.

I think that we balance out so well because we are great at CHILLING OUT together. We cook, play

*cards, unwind. In fact, being with Travis has taught
me to ALLOW myself to just be. It's OK. I need to
remind him of that, too, because we are both very
active and can get carried away with running around
all the time.*

What have you been most proud of since getting married?

Julie:

*That we have spent the last three years happy with
each other. We are honest and we try and practice our
vows daily. We made them up so that we could live by
them. My business is great and I am about to embark
on it full-time. My husband has put up with so much
while I just spent most of the last three years working
practically seven days a week constantly going on about
weddings. We are so strong together and settled.*

Jessica:

*My husband! He switched jobs and moved to a differ-
ent company only a couple of short months after our
wedding. It was a tough decision for him, as he had
been at his company for a number of years. It was our
first major decision for us to make together as a married couple – and he took a chance and now loves his
new job.*

Anita:

*Achieving the goals we set within the first 2 years of
our marriage e.g. getting our own home…*

It is clear that effective communication is something which all of these brides recognise as a benefit to achieving the aims of the couple. Communication is therefore important whether it relates to specific goals such as buying a house to not going to bed angry; or having a regular date night to managing finances and/or respecting that each other wants to socialise with their friends. It is efficient communication that contributes to success in these areas.

Having established that success as a couple closely relates to how effective communication between the two is, it becomes even more important not to get caught up in communications related *faux-pas*, which is why the next section of this chapter is an integral part of the discussion.

Furthermore, now that it is standard to communicate via text, Skype and social media as well as the more 'traditional' methods – understanding potential pitfalls of this new communication becomes essential, so pay attention to the next section of this chapter.

The new communications rules: thanks to new media

> *"What's not so great is that all this technology is destroying our social skills. Not only have we given up on writing letters to each other, we barely even talk to each other. People have become so accustomed to texting that they're actually startled when the phone rings. It's like we suddenly all have Batphones. If it rings, there must be danger.*
>
> *Now we answer, "What happened? Is someone tied up in the old sawmill?"*
>
> *"No, it's Becky. I just called to say hi."*
>
> *"Well you scared me half to death. You can't just pick up the phone and try to talk to me like that. Don't the tips of your fingers work?"*

Ellen DeGeneres

It is not surprising that effective communication is important in striving towards a happy and supportive marriage (which is essential, so that individuals in the partnership can pursue their career goals). But now that there is such a range of platforms for communication, we need to update some of the rules.

No longer are we in an era where communication comprises discussion in person, in writing (by post or email) or over the phone. Instead, our plethora of options includes Skype, text messaging, Facebook, Twitter, Instagram and more – which means it is a valuable exercise to understand this new playing field, and learn from some mistakes couples can make due to this new level of easy accessibility with our contacts.

In my research on the topic, I came across The Social Media Couple (aka K. Jason and Kelli Krafsky). The Krafskys are nationally-recognised specialists in social media and relationships. They write and speak to help people balance technology and their relationships, use common sense and set healthy guard rails for their marriages, families and relationships in this social media age. They are the authors of *Facebook and Your Marriage* (2010), have co-written many articles on the topic and are often sought out by media on 'techlationship' related issues. They live in the Greater Seattle area with their four kids. Their many articles include one on how 'what happens on Facebook can ruin a marriage'.

"Facebook doesn't ruin marriages, people do."

This is the most popular comment on any online news story about how social networks affect marriages.

We should know. Being the co-authors of *Facebook and Your Marriage*, we're quoted and referenced in hundreds of articles and stories about social media and relationships and the "Facebook doesn't wreck relationships, people using Facebook does" or some equivalent is posted in the comments almost every time.

No duh! No one is blaming the website itself for marital break ups. No one claims that Mark Zuckerberg is conspiring to wreak relationship havoc on the world.

Having spent the last four years observing and studying the phenomenon of how relationships are impacted by people's online habits, there's something different about Facebook.

In a recent Wall Street Journal article, we were quoted on one reason why this is:

"Affairs happen with a lightning speed on Facebook … In the real world, office romances and out-of-town trysts can take months or even years to develop. On Facebook, they happen in just a few clicks. The social network is different from most social networks or dating sites in that it both re-connects old flames and allows people to 'friend' someone they may only met once in passing. It puts temptation in the path of people who would never in a million years risk having an affair."

Add to this that people feel bolder behind a screen than in person, people still foolishly believe that "what happens on Facebook, stays on Facebook," people type and press 'Send' faster than common sense can kick in, and people feed off the rush they're feeling rather than rationally thinking about what they're doing. This is a recipe for disaster, and it happens at quantum speed on Facebook.

Based on all our work in this field, here are the top eight ways Facebooking spouses wreck their marriage on the popular social network.

1. **Traipsing down memory lane with an ex-flame:** Finding an old crush, hook-up, or boyfriend/girlfriend on Facebook is really easy. Reaching out to a past love interest and reminiscing about the "good 'ol times" recalls the feelings for one or both of the people. The longer the jaunt down memory lane, the better the chances that an emotional or physical affair will occur.

2. **Letting Facebook dominate every waking moment of the day:** The smart phone allows people to be a few thumb clicks away from Facebook and access their News Feed anyplace, anytime. This in turn can feed an addictive personality and create a sort of co-dependency with the site. Unrealistically comparing the new and exciting information people are posting online with the drab and boring life from one's own real-time existence can create all kinds of problems.

3. **Airing dirty laundry via status updates:** The "What's on your mind" question in the Status Update box is there as a suggestion, not a command. Relationships have good times and

bad times. Using Facebook to announce marriage problems, debate marital issues or rant on a spouse is only going to make a conflicted relationship more "complicated".

4. **Over sharing on relationship problems with others through chat:** Divulging marriage issues through a private, real time interaction with someone other than your spouse creates intimacy with that person. Depending on the motives of one or both people in the chat session, things can quickly evolve from sharing about a current, bad marriage to setting a foundation for starting a new relationship.

5. **Caring for online citizens in Cityville or virtual animals in Farmville more than real time family and spouse:** Playing games on Facebook is wildly popular. The excitement of the online game, the notification of new resources to help advance in the digital game, and the exchange of items for the game can leave real-time families and spouses wanting time and attention.

6. **Flirting on public posts, pictures and profiles:** Commenting is a part of the Facebook culture. Watching what you post (and how it comes across to others) is part of online etiquette. Ensuring that comments are not inappropriate is a part of personal decency. Flirting with no one but your spouse is a part of fulfilling the wedding vows.

7. **Friending people who directly or indirectly threaten the marriage:** The Facebook log in page says "Facebook helps you connect and share with the people in your life." Depending on who the people in your past and current life are, this could

be a good thing or a bad thing. And if they have a negative effect on a marriage, it's even worse. These include, but are not limited to: exes, negative influences, flirts, wacky family members, and crude friends.

8. **Refusing to talk about what happens on Facebook with spouse:** Facebook is no longer a topic for "water cooler" discussions, it is the water cooler. If it is something everyone is talking about, and where people spend a considerable amount of time each day, why shut your spouse out of this part of your life? Taking Facebook off the table for discussion indicates that there could be something that someone is hiding. Stonewalling on Facebook (or any other issue) is fatal for a marriage.

Facebook is a primary means of daily communication and is a part of most people's daily lives. Therefore, Facebook needs to be a regular discussion item for couples. In addition to friending exes and sharing passwords, other topics to include in the conversation include personal guard rails, online boundaries for your relationship, and accountability. (If you need help on this, an entire section in *Facebook and Your Marriage* walks couples through talking through these issues.) Let the Facebook topic help you connect and share with your spouse.

Whatever it takes, don't let what happens on Facebook ruin your marriage.

Original article at: http://techlationships.com/2012/05/23/what-happens-on-facebook-can-ruin-a-marriage/

Even when you think you have gotten to grips with the pros and cons of social media communications for couples, something changes, which is why Jason and Kelli then went on to explain further in a September 2011 press release:

Social Media Experts Warn Couples to Have a Face-to-Face about Facebook's Timeline Sooner Versus Later

Facebook has frequently been indicted by many scorned lovers and betrayed spouses for causing their relationship woes and broken marriages. But, the newest feature from the popular social network called *Timeline* could expose things one partner doesn't want the other to know, or reveal things to the world about their relationship that were meant to be private.

Every couple should have a sit down to discuss how their virtual life and online relationships affect their real-time marriage, according to K. Jason and Kelli Krafsky, a husband and wife duo who specialize in how technology impacts relationships.

"With the introduction of Facebook's *Timeline* feature, users will be able to scroll through a story of your life via your past status updates, pictures and other postings," says K. Jason Krafsky, co-author of *Facebook and Your Marriage.* "Let's just say that things are going to get a lot more personal for the 800-million Facebook users, and many relationships will be exposed and made more vulnerable."

"Over the last several years, a lot of married Facebookers jumped onto the popular social network with reckless abandon and began friending people and posting updates," says Kelli Krafsky, blogger and co-speaker on social media issues. **"*Timeline* is a game changer that will put everything out there, like a digital scrapbook of your life for anyone and everyone to see. The good, the bad and the ugly."**

Based on the countless stories of heart ache and heart break, the Krafskys developed *"The Techlationship Talk,"* five questions to help couples discuss their virtual activities and technology habits to avoid causing problems in **"The Techlationship Talk" questions include:**

Is anybody not acceptable? Discuss what past and present associations are off limits to be Facebook Friends.

Is any time off limits? Share times of the day (or night) that should be free from socializing online.

Is anywhere out-of-bounds? Talk about comfort levels using private, online communication with people, including exes, flirts, or online-only friends.

Is anything taboo? Chat about what is and is not appropriate to share about one another and your relationship.

Is anyplace not allowed? Hash out situations when it is not okay to check your Facebook, such as date nights, meal times and special occasions.

"The ultimate goal of *'The Techlationship Talk'* is to spark an honest dialogue that helps couples discover where technology and their relationship converge," says Kelli.

"The social media age we live in, and especially with the Facebook's *Timeline* feature, [mean that] **couples must talk about their online habits and how their virtual worlds and real worlds collide**," says Jason, "because like it or not, they do."

http://techlationships.com/2011/09/27/social-media-experts-warn-couples-to-have-a-face-to-face-about-facebook%E2%80%99s-timeline-sooner-versus-later/

Couples Communication Exercise 2: Establish your own communication rules

What are my favourite tips for effective communication in marriage? (Incorporate the above or share your own)

1. _____
   _____
   _____
   _____

2. _____
   _____
   _____

3. _____
   _____
   _____
   _____

Consider this:

Why do I think effective communication between couples is essential for effective career development and progress?

_____
_____
_____
_____

Why do I think effective communication between couples is essential on a personal level?

_____
_____
_____
_____

The Social Media Couple's book, *Facebook and Your Marriage*, is a book that deals less with Facebook how-tos and more about relationship how-to's, and has guided many couples through the numerous social network-related issues they face and provides practical solutions to create online guard rails and healthy boundaries for their relationship. The Krafskys write about technology and relationship issues at their blog: http://Techlationships.com – and seem likely to be a great source of information as communication platforms evolve.

Final thought about setting your own rules of communication

Jerry Springer, renowned American talk show host, is not generally someone mentioned when it comes to healthy relationships. However, his final thought in each pro-gramme was "Take care of yourself and each other" – a valid notion for those of us in relationships.

This chapter has emphasised how important it is to communicate effectively as a couple – and how setting your own rules of communication is an integral part of that process. The advent of new media platforms like social media is just another reason why having your own agreements in place is essential.

What works for one couple may not work for another, but in this chapter there is no shortage of things for you to try – so enjoy the process of setting your own com-munications rules. The ultimate aim is to make you a consistently strong unit and that in itself makes it worth the attempt to see what works for you.

Chapter 8

Your Strength in numbers: Share Experiences

> *"The real act of marriage takes place in the heart, not in the ballroom or church or synagogue. It's a choice you make – not just on your wedding day, but over and over again – and that choice is reflected in the way you treat your husband or wife."*
>
> Barbara de Angelis

I t's interesting. Many articles and blogs which discuss how to get past the post-wedding blues refer to immediate things you can do after the big day. You know the ones, write your thank you cards, throw a post-honeymoon party, and relive the day by watching the DVD etc. These are certainly useful suggestions in their own right, but this book is designed to guide you beyond the immediate days and weeks beyond your big day. It aims to help ascertain some of the wider perspective actions that will make the shift from any blues or lows experienced after wedding fever has died down, to elation and practicality (in the most fun sense of the word!) about your future together. Quotes like the one above which reflect that marriage is a daily choice are always welcome reminders of that fact.

With that in mind, we embark on the final step in this post-wedding guide for newlyweds. Here, we will share experiences – in this instance with other newly marrieds who have wisdom to share from their own wedding and early marriage journey.

By the end of this chapter you will have:

- Received some pre-wedding top tips from new-lyweds – the kinds of things many brides would have loved to hear before their big day!
- Gained some very personal insights into post-wed-ding tips from brides around the world – some of whom experienced the post-wedding blues, some of whom didn't – but all with some useful tips to share
- An appreciation for these brides who have shared their insights with you!

Top Three Pre-wedding tips from fellow newlyweds

Elizabeth, London (via California)

1. *Enjoy it! It's a special time in life and while things can admittedly get stressful, it would be a shame to have any unnecessary stress overtake the happiness. Sometimes this means making compromises you may not have expected to, but it's far more enjoy-able to focus on the purpose of the day, which is to celebrate your union, than to get hung up on details you won't care about several years down the line.*

2. *Focus on what's meaningful to the two of you, and how you want to express your relationship. This usually doesn't take the form of the most expensive option. However, if you find yourself really wanting something that is on the high end of your budget one trick we found that worked was getting another family member to negotiate with a vendor on our behalf. That way, we weren't slaves to the intersection between emotion and finance, and in every case we wound up with something we wanted, or something even better than expected.*

3. *People want to be there for you, so let them in and let them be a part of it. There's no shortage of ways people can help you before, during and even after the wedding. They want to be a part of your story, and you'll also have a richer experience for it too.*

Priyanka, India

1. *Be calm.*

2. *Understand your husband and his family before taking any quick decisions.*

3. *Don't lose your identity.*

Shazmin, Kenya

1. *Enjoy every second of your wedding (first and foremost). Take in all the little details, savour the moments and live your dream (and forget what's*

*not right) so that when you look back, you only
have good memories of the day.*

2. *Split your honeymoon into one main and two or
   three short getaways so you can get some alone
   and down time – it's a great way to take away the
   post-wedding blues.*

3. *The first year will be the hardest….always remember its US and not ME now.*

Salma, UK

1. *Do not seek validation. It is your wedding and
   no one else's. It will be perfect for YOU no matter
   what.*

2. *Do what you feel is right for YOU – don't be prepared to alter plans for other people.*

3. *Don't lose sight of why you are getting married.
   Those silly little details you spend months stressing
   over won't matter one tiny bit on the day…*

What are your top 3 post-wedding tips to other brides?

Looking beyond the big day, main post-wedding tips that
I would share, beyond what has already been discussed in
previous chapters are:

1. **Support each other**: Be each other's biggest
    cheerleader when the times are good… and a
    most reliable pillar of support when they are
    less so. On a personal level, I love being by

my husband's side on a daily basis to celebrate achievements great and small and love that he feels the same way regarding my aspirations. We jokingly refer to each other as 'partners in crime' and the strong support which goes both ways gives us immense confidence when it comes to achieving our career and other goals.

In a career and individual aspiration sense – this support is invaluable. Whether it's volunteering at a community fundraising event, going to family members' birthdays, attending various business and marketing seminars together, brainstorming ideas for our businesses and more – the fact that we are working in partnership in the varying aspects of our lives is what builds a solid foundation for our future.

While highs and lows are a part of life, this team that we build – consciously and unconsciously – is what makes us feel like we can take on the world together. And when you feel that way, the initial post-wedding blues you may feel soon become a thing of the past!

2.   **Enjoy a spa day together**: There's nothing quite like lazing around enjoying a swim and a sauna and then having a lovely meal together. Spoil yourselves.

3.   **Set shared medium term goals**: The wedding was a major project you worked on together, now it's time to focus on some other significant projects for you as a pair. Are you saving up to

buy a house? Do you want to do some travelling in the next few years? Would you like to start planning a family? Or is one of you hoping to start a business that you can both play a part in building?

Some of the brides I interviewed also have a number of tips to share. Review them below and take into account any that you can relate to!

Helen, Canada

1. *Enjoy the fact that you don't have all those wedding-related 'to-do's' anymore, it should feel like a relief!*

2. *Instead of being upset that 'your day' is now over, think of all of life's milestones that you get to celebrate with your new husband.*

3. *If you started any health-related or self-improvement routines prior to getting married/in preparation for your wedding day (i.e., a new workout routine or exercise class, etc.), stick with it after the wedding.*

Jessica, USA

1. *Rediscover your interests from before you were engaged. Did you like to scrap book? Go to kickboxing classes? Bake? Now you have the time to do that! If you are really missing your wedding, use*

photos taken to create a digital or traditional scrapbook. That way, you can still be participating in your hobby and be getting a little bit of a "wedding fix" in. Getting over the wedding blues takes time, so take it day by day.

2. *Spend a day with your new husband technology-free. No computers, television, cell phones etc. Go for a hike, for a walk around the city, to a county fair, etc. It will give you time to be together without any interruptions – perhaps you haven't had time like this since your honeymoon?*

3. *Make some time for yourself. Treat yourself to a manicure, go shopping, or read a book in your local coffee shop. My husband is going away for the day in a couple of weeks. I am excited for my scheduled massage and to just take time for myself!*

Fariba, UK (via Edmonton, Canada)

1. *Get another focus! If it's not a baby, make sure you have something you can focus all that time spent dreaming, planning and crying onto something else right away – it helps to avoid a slump!*

2. *Allow yourself time to reminisce and relive moments of your wedding. We spent loads of phone conversations and visits with friends/family who'd been at the wedding just hearing their stories, their experiences of our wedding. We spent time organising our photos and looking and relooking at them,*

making an album, framing some, ordering others for other people, watching our video. The day took up so much of your time and energy; you deserve to bask in the memory of such a wonderful day.

3. *While my first tip may seem as if it contradicts this one, I would also say, if you don't go on honeymoon or, not a long one at least, just allow yourself time to breathe as well. The planning of a wedding does take a lot out of you and going back to work right away may seem like a shock. Give yourself a couple days to just breathe at home, laze around, watch telly enjoy the time you have to just not think about anything, to not have a list to attend to and not beat yourself up about it.*

Nicola, UK

1. *Enjoy the journey – this is all part of your path so just relax into it.*

2. *Appreciate each other – remember to take time out for each other.*

3. *Have a project – have something that you can focus on, utilising that free time you suddenly have will make you feel positive when you might be feeling down.*

Micaela, USA

1. *Just enjoy it, don't think too much about everything. Someone will always feel the need to tell you what you should do next or when you should have kids or how you should run your relationship, do whatever YOU want.*

2. *It's not all perfect, but remember all of the things that are great.*

3. *Have your own space, if you can.* ☺

Laura, UK:

1. *Have something to look forward to.*

2. *Enjoy each other's company and…*

3. *Plan for the next big stage in your life, whatever that may be.*

Trena, Canada (via Barbados)

1. *Make sure you connect with each other each day to chat about each other's day etc.*

2. *Don't sweat the small stuff. Learn to compromise or find other solutions.*

3. *Don't go to bed angry.*

Stacy, UK

1. *Discuss your short term goals with your husband, including the emotions attached with these.*

2. *Reconnect with your friends doing something enjoyable.*

3. *If there is any way you can, try to ensure money isn't your immediate concern.*

Sharmeen, USA

1. *Don't fall prey to others' expectations, including those by society that are ingrained in our minds, especially at the time of a wedding!*

2. *Don't sweat the details.*

3. *Lose your ego! Respect yourself and your partner. Understand you are not the same person and will have differences even in things you didn't think so. As long as he does not disrespect you, lose the ego!*

Pamela, USA

1. *Remember to invest time in doing things together, just the two of you.*

2. *Dress up for your hubby and surprise him with little things here and there.*

3. *And, don't get lazy in the relationship! Talk. Kiss. Date each other, etc.*

Bethan, UK

1. *Don't expect things to change massively. You were happy before, that's why you agreed to get married in the first place!*

2. *Enjoy talking about the past together, but always keep a keen eye on the future. Your wedding was amazing, but there will be plenty more amazing things up ahead as well.*

3. *Expect bad wife jokes…for life…!*

Lexi, UK

1. *Put any feelings of disappointment into perspective. What you have gained is far more valuable than what you perceive you have lost.*

2. *Understand that nothing has to change. You got engaged based on your lives together at that point so why change what led you to walk up the aisle.*

3. *It's hard, but it's ultimately worth fighting for. If there is something external that is affecting your lives together then it needs to be dealt with. Try to find compromise where possible but if not then assess what would happen if you had to back down.*

Happily Ever After For Grown-Ups

Jeannine, Jamaica/Canada

1. *Maintain a few things that made you "you" before you met him (name, hobbies, beauty rituals, friends…etc). Remember that he fell in love with you as you were.*

2. *Remember that post-wedding blues will eventually fade. Don't question your entire marriage on your emotions during that period of time. Trust your decision.*

3. *Prioritize intimate time together to keep the spark alive.*

Julie, UK

1. *Enjoy your free time from wedding planning. Use the extra time to put into your relationship or career or both.*

2. *Arrange a weekend away together a few months after the wedding to take stock and spend time together.*

3. *Realise that if you do feel the blues, it will be transient and you will certainly pass through them.*

And with these fantastic insights from a selection of brides based around the world, the only thing left to do now is go forth and enjoy the next steps, post-marriage.

I hope you agree that taking the time to share experiences with a non-judgemental approach goes a long way towards achieving the desired motivation to pursue both "me" and "we" focused goals… therefore bringing you a touch closer to a realistic and exciting journey towards 'happily ever after'.

Chapter 9

Meet the contributors

From top tips on conducting self and career audits to setting the rules for communication in marriage, I hope this book has not only provided food for thought but also given you some tangible ideas that you can put into practice in a bid to successfully reach your goals as individuals and as a couple.

As personal stories of brides and expert contributions of professionals in the wedding and coaching business have been an instrumental part of this book, I would like to share some of their biographies and key messages here... and where relevant, indicate where you can access more information from them.

Jeannine Archer-Duhaney MD

Jeannine Archer is a doctor who relocated from Canada to Jamaica after her December 2010 wedding. Married for two happy years and counting, for her marriage was always about partnership. Two individuals becoming stronger once they loved each other and worked together. "It is something that I saw in my parents growing up and definitely always wanted for myself." She is a mum of one and believes in working to live...not living to work!

Helen Burnett-Nichols

Helen Burnett-Nichols (www.burnettnichols.com) is a freelance journalist who has written everything from entertainment to financial news and features for international, national and local print and online publications over the last eight years. Based in Hamilton, Ontario, Canada, Helen married her husband Paul in 2006 and recently became a mum to Grant. She continues to strive to find a balance between her increasingly busy family life and her evolving career.

Lexi Couchman

Lexi Couchman (known under her maiden name Jarman, professionally) works in the media, in a 'creative solutions' sales role. She describes herself as being very active in her career development during before her wedding as she was pursuing a new role on a different team full time (business development/creative solutions rather than display ad sales). She applied for and was then offered a new position at work during the period that she was engaged. Her last day in her old position was the week before her wedding day and she started her new position fresh from their honeymoon.

Married in 2010, she believes that it is important to work on your relationship as well as your career because the two are interdependent. "As both are such large (yet separate) areas of your life, anything that is wrong in either will naturally be detrimental to the other if not careful. The two should support each other and not compete; otherwise the balance could cause permanent damage to your relationship or your career."

Julie Dawson

Julie Dawson is known as "The Wedding Planner", a reflection of the career she moved into after getting married in 2008. Based in the West Midlands (UK), Julie says it is "important to wake up each day happy with my husband, you have to work on that it doesn't just happen. My business is about people getting married, I want to be a good role model for a happy balanced married life. I need it for me too; my partner is my best friend, confidante and voice of reason." You can access Julie's wedding planning services on www.theweddinggenie.co.uk and www.theweddinggenie.co.uk/blog.

Trena Isaac

Trena Issac married her best friend Sunil Issac in July 2009. She is from the little island of Barbados, but currently residing in Toronto, Canada for the last 10 years.

After graduating from York University with a psychology degree and vocational rehabilitation certificate, she ended up working for the insurance company where she had completed her coop student placement, and has been there for the past six and half years as an Accident Benefits analyst. With her desire to help others and share knowledge, she has been a mentor to junior colleagues within her department, and is currently exploring other roles that would allow her more opportunity to foster this desire.

Trena strongly agrees that when she was planning her wedding, she focused less on her career development than she otherwise would have, partly due to being involved in a long distance relationship at the time and planning a wedding in another country! She recognised that she would spend more time on her career development after the wedding and when things settled down.

Sharmeen Jariullah

Sharmeen Jariullah is a makeup artist with a background in psychology and an interest in working with under-represented communities. Based in Chicago, Illinois (USA) she thinks think that women now live in a world where we are expected to accomplish much more than ever expected before. She believes this has many positives for women but recognises that one of the things society and fairy tales has told us is that relationships work themselves out. She stresses this is "Not true... We cannot forget to focus on ourselves and also on our relationships, especially in marriage when it comes to that level of commitment that has been made. It will not be roses and fairy tales every day so love, respect and comprise must prevail. Yet those things don't come without some effort and as women focus on working hard at our careers, we have to do the same in our personal lives, for our own sake :)"

You can connect with Sharmeen at pinterest.com/SharJar

Shazmin Manji

Shazmin Manji is the Product Development Manager and Retail Travel Manager for family business Twiga Tours, based in Nairobi, Kenya. She is a specialist in luxury and bespoke holidays within East Africa & beyond, including private charters, private island retreats, luxury villa escapes and more. In addition, she is an experienced event organiser and owner of Mimba Enterprise, Kenya's first specialised maternity wear shop. With a double barrelled name in her personal life, Shazmin Manji-Karmali is a busy, happy, married mum of one who believes in balancing it all (and notoriously walked into her office on the morning of her wedding but swiftly retreated after her colleagues insisted she left to give full attention to her special day)!

Carolina Massie

Carolina Massie was a Movement Director and Actor before marriage. Based in Munich and married in June 2010, she continued working in the Arts until her son was born and is now a full-time Mum. She thinks both career and your relationship are important. Her work was something she massively identified with and giving it up has been difficult. However, she recognises that "my husband and I always wanted kids and we are a good team, having a baby cemented our ability to work together."

Pamela Mellott

Pamela Mellott is a small business owner and marketing consultant based in Columbia, Maryland (USA). She got married to husband Brandon in November 2010 strongly agrees that she spent less time focused on her career development during the wedding planning process than she ordinarily would have. She moved jobs about 6 months after the wedding and describes herself as a "marketing director by day with dreams of becoming a stay at home wife and mommy at night". Visit her on her blog www.ourlovenestblog.com

Stacy Moore

Stacy Moore lives in London and married Charles in June 2011. She is a chartered educational psychologist, who just prior to her wedding took the decision to leave full time local authority work and establish her own company, Inner Circles Educational Psychology. 18 months on, she is enjoying providing consultation, training and assessments in a range of community settings (see www.innercircles.org.uk).

Stacy thinks it is important to work on your relationship as well as your career because the partnership you've decided to form with your spouse isn't a 9 - 5 with overtime where you may look forward to retiring; your relationship will nurture you, provide emotional support and self-esteem way beyond office hours, and hopefully way past your 60th or 65th birthday! If you're lucky, your relationship will outlive any career goals you set for yourself and influence the direction of your professional and personal development.

Nicola Rae-Wickham

Nicola got married in 2011 and worked as a marketing officer both before and after the wedding. Since getting married, she has started the blog mentioned below, is working on setting up her own marketing consultancy, and has started a 9 month post graduate course.

Inspired by her own wedding, she launched the wedding blog for black British brides: BelleNoirBride. Combining her love of weddings with her marketing communications background, she has created a resource she would have valued during her own wedding planning. BelleNoirBride has its foundations as a wedding blog and aims to provide bridal inspiration for all in a way the main stream publications are failing to do. In addition it is also a journey through life, style and love. Visit www.bellenoirbride.co.uk

Bella Rareworld

Bella Rareworld from BellaNetworking Events Ltd is the Networking Guru. She takes professional networking to another level working as a Networking Specialist. Bella specialises in strategic networking helping business owners, SMEs and employers to see faster networking result by building high impact quality network base. She also works closely with women, teaching them how to use networking when job hunting and to achieve career goals. Bella works on a one to one basis or group training, her style focuses on goal-setting. Bella has a natural energy and passion for networking, as is evident in the networking tips she shared for newlyweds in this book. You can find out more about her here www.bellanetworking.com and http://www.linkedin.com/in/rareworld

Fariba Soetan

Fariba Soetan is a policy advisor in the civil service. Based in Bristol in the west of the UK, Fariba is originally from Canada. Married in May 2010, she then got pregnant, had a year off then went back to work and got a promotion to senior higher education policy adviser (civil service). She strongly agrees that when she was planning her wedding, she focused less on her career development than she otherwise would have and describes the post-wedding blues as the time when the high of planning one of the biggest days of your life is over. It is when all the energy, time, motivation, emotion that went into planning that one event has reached a climax and now it's over and now you have no outlet for it all. What do you do with all that time, emotion, and energy you invested now? To avoid a slump, she recommends finding a new focus so you can channel all that time spent dreaming and planning.

Erin Tillman

Erin Tillman is known as The Dating Advice Girl. Based in Los Angeles, California her mission is to help singles get the most out of the single life, without losing themselves in the dating process. In her capacity as a Dating Expert/ Single Life Consultant, she was the perfect person to contribute date ideas for newlyweds and more information about Erin is available here www.TheDatingAdviceGirl.com

Karen Williams

Karen Williams is a Business Coach, firewalk instructor, speaker and trainer, and has been running her business, Self Discovery Coaching since 2006. The author of two successful business books, she specialises in working with solopreneurs who are breaking free from the corporate world and want to create a successful business, stand out from the crowd and enjoy every step of the way. She was inspired to set up her business when she sought her own coach in January 2006, just a few months after getting married. She woke up one day and realised that she no longer enjoyed her job and needed to do something different, and with coaching she found her passion. You can find out more about Karen at www.selfdiscoverycoaching.co.uk.

Chapter **10**

Next Steps

"*The modern fairytale ending is the reverse of the traditional one: A woman does not wait for Prince Charming to bring her happiness; she lives happily ever after only by refusing to wait for him – or by actually rejecting him. It is those who persist in hoping for a Prince Charming who are setting themselves up for disillusionment and unhappiness.*"

Susan Faludi

Over the course of the last nine chapters, I have tried to bring the notion 'happily ever after' off the pages of our favourite fairytales and into the real world.

It needed to be poked at, prodded, challenged, explored and redefined… and in this book, I aimed to highlight the unrealistic nature of this somewhat flimsy ideal. I aspired to create a blueprint of steps towards realistically achieving a modern day version of this misleadingly simple sentiment, which has been a part of our consciousness since childhood.

"When a couple initially gets together, it involves two individuals being attracted to the qualities that each other possess. It therefore stands to reason that an important aspect of remaining part of a happy partnership is to be happy and fulfilled as individuals. To that end, focusing on our own personal and professional aspirations and goals is a must – while simultaneously always, ALWAYS working as a team."

Gina Visram

Life does not consist of Cinderella waiting for her Prince Charming, Beauty transforming her Beast, or Jasmine being swept away on a magic carpet by her Aladdin. And nor should it. What it does involve however is a series of exciting decisions and challenges. And when we are at the relationship, newlywed and marriage stage – making decisions that benefit the individual *and* the couple. Compromise will always be necessary when two people form such a partnership – however I hope that as long as communication is clear and shared, agreed goals are consistently the vision – we can realistically live the lives we dreamed of.

"Marriage is not a noun; it's a verb. It isn't something you get. It's something you do. It's the way you love your partner every day."

Barbara De Angelis

At this stage, I think it's important for me to reiterate that I do not see myself as a relationship expert. I am still a newlywed and wouldn't dare to be that presumptuous. What I am proud to be however is a career and success coach who is dedicated to working with clients as they embark on some of the most exciting times of their lives. My mission is to help those I work with to achieve career and personal goals, make the most of their potential and not get in their own way!

It was my own experience as a newlywed who was (still is and will hopefully always be) incredibly in love with her husband. I'm thrilled to be married to the person I wanted to share my life's adventures with – yet nonetheless I felt inexplicably 'blah' for a short while and that made me embark on the journey of writing this book. In those weeks following our wedding ceremonies, I knew I was not at my best, due to (what I later realised was) a post-wedding blues slump in motivation.

This, despite the fact that:

- I was not a bride who was unhealthily fixated on her wedding day (as opposed to her marriage). I worked to create a special day but was incredibly excited about the marriage and our future together.
- I had successfully kept on top of my career development during my engagement period.

Contrary to what some may think when they comment on (rare) blogs about the post-wedding blues, it is *not* exclusive to women who have lost perspective! The real life stories are too rich and varied for that to be the case, which is why I am excited to have embarked on this project. Conversations with friends, acquaintances, people online with shared interests and the real stories in this book highlight that this 'slump' can take varying guises but a shift to married status is an important one for individuals and for couples and it was important to open up this dialogue. Although everyone has different experiences, the common factor is that everyone I spoke to was interested in hearing more and understanding the experiences of others.

The coaching approach is always great, and really was the best approach here due to those differences in experience. I know that you don't want someone telling you what to do as they don't know your life – only you know that! Instead, the non-directive, coaching approach meant that over the course of the chapters in this book, you could work out your own path towards whatever you define as success, while perhaps being inspired by the experiences of others.

More happily ever after for grown-ups

This book is just part of the journey. You've now read about and started the process of doing a self-audit, sharpening your goal setting skills, reconnecting with your networks, strengthening your partnership, conducting a career audit, exploring couple communication and sharing experiences.

Moving forward, please don't hesitate to contact me about one-on-one coaching (on Skype or in person); group coaching and workshops, webinars, CDs, audio content and much more. Contact me to find out more about the next "Happily Ever After for Grown Ups" workshops or teleseminar… you can join me from wherever you are in the world.

I am always proud to work with people who are determined to live up to their potential as they embark on some of the most exciting times of their lives and are determined to make active decisions to not get in their own way!

Please do connect with me in a range of ways, including by email (gina@limitlesscoaching.com); on Twitter @ bridemotivation and @limitlesscoach; and online www.post-wedding.com and www.limitlesscoaching.com

Final thought

Essentially, if you make the shift from talking about your wedding as "the best day of my life" – to instead saying "one of the best days of my life" you are suddenly giving yourself room for a plethora of other amazing days in the future. You have all kinds of exciting personal and professional goals you'd like to achieve as you strive to work towards the lifestyle you see for yourself – and there are some exciting times ahead.

Bring it on…

References and Further Reading, Further Listening and Further Watching

Alam-Naylor, S. (May 2011), *The English Wedding Blog*, On the Other Side, http://english-wedding.com/2011/05/on-the-other-side/

Ardolino, E. (Director) *Dirty Dancing*. (1987) Perfs: Jennifer Grey, Patrick Swayze. Lions Gate

Azim, R. Benson, H. (November 2012) The Marriage Foundation: *Hello? Goodbye! Marriage and divorce among celebrities*, http://www.marriagefoundation.org.uk/Web/News/News.aspx?news=127&RedirectUrl=%2fWeb%2fContent%2fDefault.aspx%3fContent%3d27

Canfield, J. (2006) *The Success Principles*(TM): How to Get from Where You Are to Where You Want to Be

Dwyer Hogg, C. (2009) "Should women trade in their surname when they get married?", *The Independent*, http://www.independent.co.uk/life-style/love-sex/marriage/should-women-trade-in-their-surname-when-they-get-married-1717794.html

Gordon, M. & Warren H, (1960) *At Last* (sung by Etta James)

Whitworth, L Kimsey-House, K. Kimsey-House, H. Sandahl, P. (2007) *Co-Active Coaching: New Skills for Coaching People Toward Success in Work and Life (2nd Edition)*

Please note: There is a newer version of this book for your reference:

Kimsey-House, K. Kimsey-House, H. Sandahl, P. Whitworth, L (2011) *Co-Active Coaching: Changing Business, Transforming Lives (3rd Edition)*

Krafsky, J. & Krafsky, K. (a.k.a. The Social Media Couple), *Facebook doesn't ruin marriages, people do* & *Social Media Experts Warn Couples to Have a Face-to-Face about Facebook's Timeline Sooner Versus Later* – both reproduced from http://techlationships.com/ with permission from the authors

Landis, J. (Director) *Coming to America.* (1988) Perfs: Eddie Murphy, Arsenio Hall. Paramount Pictures - Excerpt from COMING TO AMERICA © 1988 BY Paramount Pictures. All Rights Reserved.

Merriam Webster dictionary online - http://www.merriam-webster.com/dictionary/goal

Mills, J. Suffering post-wedding blues? *Daily Mail.* Retrieved from www.dailymail.co.uk

Mindtools.com, Locke's Goal Setting Theory: Understanding SMART Goal Setting, http://www.mindtools.com/pages/article/newHTE_87.htm, retrieved November 2011; © Mind Tools Ltd, 1996-2013. All rights reserved. «Reproduced with permission

Office for National Statistics, 20 December 2012, Statistical bulletin: *Divorces in England and Wales 2011*, http://www.ons.gov.uk/ons/rel/vsob1/divorces-in-england-and-wales/2011/stb-divorces-2011.html

Oxford English Dictionary online - http://oxford dictionaries.com/definition/english/marriage

Richie, L. (1992), *My Destiny*

Robbins, A. (2001) *Awaken the Giant Within*, page 47

Shakespeare, W. Act 2, Scene 2, *Romeo and Juliet*, www.shakespeare-online.com

Visram, G. (November 2011), *The Secrets of Effective Job Hunting*, The Voice, http://www.voice-online.co.uk/career-education-article/secrets-effective-job-hunting